Collins

Unlocking ITALIAN

with

Paul Noble

Published by Collins
An imprint of HarperCollins Publishers
Westerhill Road
Bishopbriggs
Glasgow G64 2QT

HarperCollins Publishers
Macken House
39/40 Mayor Street Upper
Dublin 1 D01 C9W8 Ireland

First edition 2017

10 9 8 7 6 5

© Paul Noble 2017

ISBN 978-0-00-813584-3
US ISBN 978-0-00-854721-9

Collins® is a registered trademark of
HarperCollins Publishers Limited

Typeset by Davidson Publishing Solutions,
Glasgow

Printed in Italy by Grafica Veneta S.p.A.

A catalogue record for this book is available
from the British Library.

If you would like to comment on any aspect
of this book, please contact us at the given
address or online.
E-mail dictionaries@harpercollins.co.uk
www.facebook.com/collinsdictionary
@collinsdict

Acknowledgements
Images from Shutterstock.

MANAGING EDITOR
Maree Airlie

CONTRIBUTORS
Francesca Logi
Janice McNeillie
Maggie Seaton
Val McNulty

FOR THE PUBLISHER
Gerry Breslin
Holly Tarbet
Kevin Robbins
Vaila Donnachie

People who know no Italian at all

People who know some Italian already

People who studied Italian at school

People who didn't study Italian at school

People who didn't like how languages were taught at school

People who are amazed by just how closely grammar
books resemble furniture assembly instructions

Who is this book for?

People who think they can't learn a foreign language

People who've listened to one of Paul Noble's audio courses

People who haven't listened to one of Paul Noble's audio courses

People learning Italian for the first time

People coming back to the language after a break

People curious about whether they can learn a language

**People who feel confused by the way languages
are normally taught**

Contents

Did you know you
already speak Italian?

Did you know you already speak Italian?

That you speak it every day? That you read and write it every day? That you use it with your friends, with your family, at work, down the post-office – even in the shower when you read the label on the shampoo bottle?

Were you aware of that fact?

Well, even if you weren't, it's nevertheless true.

Of course, you might not have realised at the time that what you were reading / saying / writing was actually Italian but I can prove to you that it was. Just take a look at these Italian words below but, as you do so, use your thumb to cover the final letter at the end of each word:

importante	romantico	urgente	sarcasmo
normale	stupido	locale	concerto
tutore	recente	timido	finale

fantastico	elegante	splendido	
traffico	totale	differente	panico
intelligente	naturale		

As your thumb has hopefully helped you to realise, these are words that exist not only in Italian but also in English. And, in fact, these are by no means isolated examples of words that exist in both Italian and English but rather they are merely the tip of a *truly enormous* iceberg.

In fact, around half of all English words have close equivalents in Italian. Yes, that's right, *half!*

If we begin using these words, together with an extremely subtle method that shows you how to put them into sentences in a way that's almost effortless, then becoming a competent Italian speaker becomes really quite easy.

The only thing that *you* will need to do to make this happen is to follow the three simple rules printed on the following pages. These rules will explain to you how to use this book so that you can begin unlocking the Italian language for yourself in a matter of hours.

well, What are you Waiting for?
Turn the page!

Rule Number 1:

Don't skip anything!

Using this book is extremely simple – and highly effective – *if* you follow its three simple rules.

If you don't want to follow them, then I recommend that, instead of reading the book, you use it to prop up a wobbly coffee table, as it won't work if you don't follow the rules. Now get ready – because here's the first one!

Each and every little thing in this book has been put where it is, in a very particular order, for a very particular reason. So, if the book asks you to read or do something, then do it! Who's the teacher after all, you or me, eh?

Also, each part of the book builds on and reinforces what came before it. If you start skipping sections, you will end up confused and lost. Instead, you should just take your time and gently work your way through the book at your own pace – *but without skipping anything!*

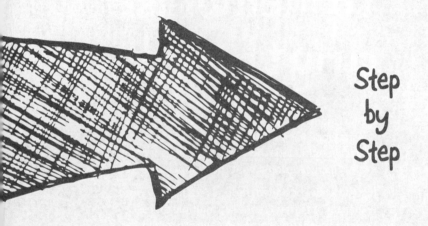

Step
by
Step

Rule Number 2:
Don't try to memorise anything!

Trying to jam things into your head is boring *and* it doesn't work. People often cram for tests and then forget everything the moment they walk out of the exam. Clearly, we don't want that happening here.

Instead, I have designed this book so that any word or idea taught in it will come up multiple times. You don't need to worry about trying to remember or memorise anything because the necessary repetition is actually already built in. In fact, trying to memorise what you're learning is likely to hinder rather than help your progress.

So, just work your way through the book in a relaxed way and, if you happen to forget something, don't worry because, as I say, you will be reminded of it again, multiple times, later on.

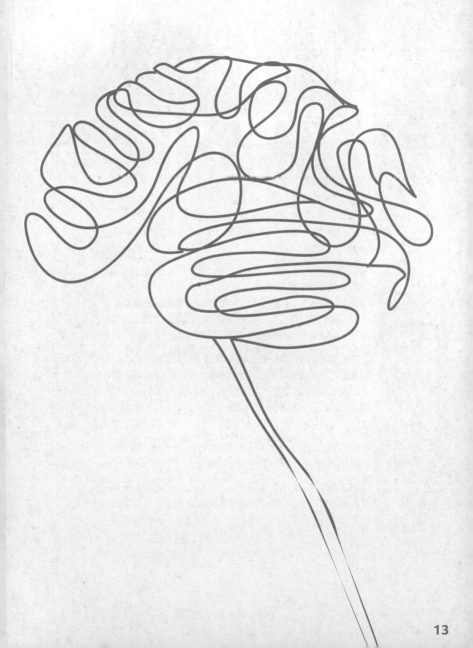

Rule Number 3:
Cover up!

No, I'm not being a puritan grandmother and telling you to put on a long-sleeved cardigan. Instead, I'm asking you to take a bookmark or piece of paper and use it to cover up any **green text** that you come across as you work your way through the book.

These **green bits** are the answers to the various riddles, challenges and questions that I will pose as I lead you into the Italian language. If you read these answers without at least trying to work out the solutions first, then the book simply won't work for you.

So, make sure to use something to cover up the bits of **green text** in the book while you have a go at trying to work out the answers. It doesn't matter if you sometimes get them wrong because it is by trying to think out the answers that you will learn how to use the language.

Trust me on this, you will see that it works from the very first page!

Take a look at the page on the right to see how to use your bookmark or piece of paper to cover up correctly.

You can now already correctly say "I have visited Rome" and "I visited Rome" because they are exactly the same in Italian. With this in mind, do you think you can make a lucky guess about how you might say "I *did* visit Rome"? Just take a wild guess!

Ho visitato Roma.
(o visit-art-oh roam-er)

Once again, it is exactly the same in Italian. "I have visited Rome", "I visited Rome" and "I did visit Rome" are all said in precisely the same way. In fact this is one of the many wonderful things about Italian: you get three English tenses for the price of one Italian one! "I have visited Rome", "I visited Rome" and "I did visit Rome" are all simply:

Ho visitato Roma.
(o visit-art-oh roam-er)

Let's try this 3 For the Price of 1 Special Offer again now but this time with a different example.

To say "I have spent" in Italian, you will literally say "I have passed", which in Italian is:

Ho passato
(o pass-art-oh)

"The weekend" in Italian is:

il weekend
(eel weekend)

So how would you say "I have spent the weekend" (literally "I have passed the weekend")?

Ho passato il weekend
(o pass-art-oh eel weekend)

And how would you say simply "I spent the weekend" / "I passed the weekend"?

Ho passato il weekend
(o pass-art-oh eel weekend)

Just as "I visited Rome" and "I have visited Rome" are no different from one another in Italian, so "I spent the weekend" and "I have spent the weekend" are also no different from one another.

How do you think you would say "I *did* spend the weekend"?

Ho passato il weekend

Make sure to cover up any green words, just like this!

(a roam-er)

So how would you say "I have spent the weekend in Rome"?

Ho passato il weekend a Roma.
(o pass-art-oh eel weekend a roam-er)

And how would you say "I spent the weekend in Rome"?

Ho passato il weekend a Roma.
(o pass-art-oh eel weekend a roam-er)

And "I did spend the weekend in Rome"?

Ho passato il weekend a Roma.
(o pass-art-oh eel weekend a roam-er)

You can now already correctly say "I have visited Rome" and "I visited Rome" because they are exactly the same in Italian. With this in mind, do you think you can make a lucky guess about how you might say "I *did* visit Rome"? Just take a wild guess!

Ho visitato Roma.
(o visit-art-oh roam-er)

Once again, it is exactly the same in Italian. "I have visited Rome", "I visited Rome" and "I did visit Rome" are all said in precisely the same way. In fact this is one of the many wonderful things about Italian: you get three English tenses for the price of one Italian one! "I have visited Rome", "I visited Rome" and "I did visit Rome" are all simply:

Ho visitato Roma.
(o visit-art-oh roam-er)

Let's try this 3 For the Price of 1 Special Offer again now but this time with a different example.

To say "I have spent" in Italian, you will literally say "I have passed", which in Italian is:

Ho passato
(o pass-art-oh)

"The weekend" in Italian is:

il weekend
(eel weekend)

So how would you say "I have spent the weekend" (literally "I have passed the weekend")?

Ho passato il weekend
(o pass-art-oh eel weekend)

20

And how would you say simply "I spent the weekend" / "I passed the weekend"?

Ho passato il weekend
(o pass-art-oh eel weekend)

Just as "I visited Rome" and "I have visited Rome" are no different from one another in Italian, so "I spent the weekend" and "I have spent the weekend" are also no different from one another.

How do you think you would say "I *did* spend the weekend"?

Ho passato il weekend
(o pass-art-oh eel weekend)

Then, having tried to work out the answer, uncover and check!

Ho passato il weekend a Roma.
(o pass-art-oh eel weekend a roam-er)

And how would you say "I spent the weekend in Rome"?

Ho passato il weekend a Roma.
(o pass-art-oh eel weekend a roam-er)

And "I did spend the weekend in Rome"?

Ho passato il weekend a Roma.
(o pass-art-oh eel weekend a roam-er)

21

CHAPTER 1

I spent the weekend in Rome —
and wow, the weather was fantastic.

> "I spent the weekend in Rome — and wow, the weather was fantastic." Not such a complicated sentence in English, is it? Or is it...?

I have taught many people over the years, ranging from those who know no Italian at all, through to those who may have studied Italian for several years at school. Yet whether they have studied the language before or not, almost none of them tend to be able to construct a basic sentence like this when I first meet them.

Admittedly, they might know how to say other far less useful things, like: "I'm 37 years old and have two sisters and a goldfish" – an unusual conversation opener from my perspective – but they can't say what they did at the weekend.

Well, in just a few minutes' time, you *will* be able to do this – even if you've never learnt any Italian before.

Just remember though: ***don't skip anything***, ***don't* waste your time trying to memorise anything** but ***do* use your bookmark to cover up anything green you find on each page.**

Okay now, let's begin!

"I have" in Italian is:

Ho
(pronounced "o"[1])

And the word for "visited" in Italian is:

visitato

With this in mind, how would you say "I have visited"?

Ho visitato
(o visit-art-oh)

⟵ Did you remember to cover up the green words while you worked out the answer?

---

1   Here's a bit of extra pronunciation guidance for you: the letter "h" is silent in Italian, so "ho" (I have) is pronounced like the "o" at the beginning of the word "odd".

"Naples" in Italian is:

Napoli
(nap-oh-lee)

So, with this in mind, how would you say "I have visited Naples"?

Ho visitato Napoli.
(o visit-art-oh nap-oh-lee)

The word for "Rome" in Italian is:

Roma
(roam-er)

So how would you say "I have visited Rome"?

Ho visitato Roma.
(o visit-art-oh roam-er)

Now, if I were to ask you how you would say simply "I visited Rome" rather than "I *have* visited Rome" you might not think you knew how to say that yet. However, you will be glad to hear that I would disagree with you because, in Italian, talking about what has happened in the past is far easier than it is in English. This is because "I visited Rome" and "I have visited Rome" are said in *exactly the same way* in Italian. I'll show you what I mean.

Again, how would you say "I have visited Rome"?

Ho visitato Roma.
(o visit-art-oh roam-er)

I want you to now try to say "I visited Rome" bearing in mind that what you're going to say is *exactly* the same as what you just said for "I have visited Rome". So, "I visited Rome" will be:

Ho visitato Roma.
(o visit-art-oh roam-er)

As you can see, it is exactly the same. Italians do not make a distinction between the two. Effectively, you have got two English past tenses for the price of one. And actually it is even better than that.

You can now already correctly say "I have visited Rome" and "I visited Rome" because they are exactly the same in Italian. With this in mind, do you think you can make a lucky guess about how you might say "I *did* visit Rome"? Just take a wild guess!

Ho visitato Roma.
(*o visit-art-oh roam-er*)

Once again, it is exactly the same in Italian. "I have visited Rome", "I visited Rome" and "I did visit Rome" are all said in precisely the same way. In fact this is one of the many wonderful things about Italian: you get three English tenses for the price of one Italian one! "I have visited Rome", "I visited Rome" and "I did visit Rome" are all simply:

Ho visitato Roma.
(*o visit-art-oh roam-er*)

Let's try this 3 For the Price of 1 Special Offer again now but this time with a different example.

To say "I have spent" in Italian, you will literally say "I have passed", which in Italian is:

Ho passato
(*o pass-art-oh*)

"The weekend" in Italian is:

il weekend
(*eel weekend*)

So how would you say "I have spent the weekend" (literally "I have passed the weekend")?

Ho passato il weekend
(*o pass-art-oh eel weekend*)

And how would you say simply "I spent the weekend" / "I passed the weekend"?

Ho passato il weekend
(o pass-art-oh eel weekend)

Just as "I visited Rome" and "I have visited Rome" are no different from one another in Italian, so "I spent the weekend" and "I have spent the weekend" are also no different from one another.

How do you think you would you say "I *did* spend the weekend"?

Ho passato il weekend
(o pass-art-oh eel weekend)

Again, you have three English past tenses for the price of one in Italian.

"I spent the weekend", "I have spent the weekend", "I did spend the weekend" – it's all the same in Italian: "Ho passato il weekend".

"In Rome" in Italian is:

a Roma
(a roam-er)

So how would you say "I have spent the weekend in Rome"?

Ho passato il weekend a Roma.
(o pass-art-oh eel weekend a roam-er)

And how would you say "I spent the weekend in Rome"?

Ho passato il weekend a Roma.
(o pass-art-oh eel weekend a roam-er)

And "I did spend the weekend in Rome"?

Ho passato il weekend a Roma.
(o pass-art-oh eel weekend a roam-er)

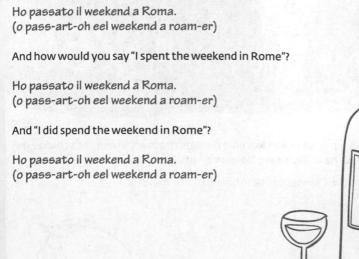

Time to steal some words!
Word Robbery Number 1

Let's forget our weekend in Rome for just one moment now and start stealing some words. Around half the words in modern English have come into our language via Latin languages, such as Italian. Once you can identify them, you will have a large, instant, usable vocabulary in Italian. After all, why bother learning Italian vocabulary when you can simply steal it?

The first group of words we are going to steal are words that end in "**ic**" and "**ical**" in English.

Words like "roman**tic**", "fantas**tic**", "polit**ical**", "illog**ical**" and so on.

There are around 750 of these in English and they are largely similar in Italian, except that in Italian they end in "**ico**" (pronounced "eek-oh"), becoming "roman**tico**", "fantas**tico**", "poli**tico**", "illog**ico**" and so on.

Let's now see how we can use these to begin expanding our range of expressions in Italian!

Words stolen so far 750

Bearing in mind what we've just learnt in the Word Robbery above, let's change the "ic" on the end of the English word "romant**ic**" into "**ico**".

Doing this, what will "romantic" be in Italian?

romantico
(roe-man-teek-oh)

And so what would "fantastic" be in Italian?

fantastico
(fan-tass-teek-oh)

Let's now try doing the same with "ical" and change the "ical" on the end of "political" into "ico".

Doing this, what will "political" be in Italian?

politico
(pol-ee-teek-oh)

And what will "illogical" be?

illogico
(ee-lodge-eek-oh)

Let's now try using these "ico" words to expand our range of expressions and to make some more complex sentences in Italian.

"It was" in Italian is:

Era
(air-ah)

So, how would you say "it was illogical"?

Era illogico.
(air-ah ee-lodge-eek-oh)

And how would you say "it was political"?

Era politico.
(air-ah pol-ee-teek-oh)

How about "it was romantic"?

Era romantico.
(air-ah roe-man-teek-oh)

Finally, how would you say "it was fantastic"?

Era fantastico.
(air-ah fan-tass-teek-oh)

Now, do you remember how to say "I have visited" in Italian?

Ho visitato
(o visit-art-oh)

And what about "I visited"?

Ho visitato
(o visit-art-oh)

And "I did visit"?

Ho visitato
(o visit-art-oh)

Do you remember how to say "I have spent", "I did spend", "I spent" (literally "I have passed")?

Ho passato
(o pass-art-oh)

And so how would you say "I spent the weekend"?

Ho passato il weekend
(o pass-art-oh eel weekend)

What is "in Rome" in Italian?

a Roma
(a roam-er)

So how would you say "I spent the weekend in Rome"?

Ho passato il weekend a Roma.
(o pass-art-oh eel weekend a roam-er)

And once more, what is "it was" in Italian?

Era
(air-ah)

Now, "era" can be used in Italian to mean both "it was" and also just "was".

"The weather" in Italian is:

il tempo
(eel tem-poe)

So how would you say "the weather was..."?

il tempo era...
(eel tem-poe air-ah)

Now again, what was "fantastic" in Italian?

fantastico
(fan-tass-teek-oh)

And so how would you say "the weather was fantastic"?

Il tempo era fantastico.
(eel tem-poe air-ah fan-tass-teek-oh)

And how would you say "I spent the weekend in Rome. The weather was fantastic."?

Ho passato il weekend a Roma. Il tempo era fantastico.
(o pass-art-oh eel weekend a roam-er. eel tem-poe air-ah fan-tass-teek-oh)

If you want to show that you're amazed or impressed by something in Italian, you can, just as in English, say "wow".

So, just to make this clear, what is "wow" in Italian?

wow
(wow)

Good.

The word for "and" in Italian is:

e
(ay)

So, how would you say "...and wow..."?

...e wow...
(ay wow)

Putting what you've learnt together, say "I spent the weekend in Rome – and wow, it was fantastic." Take your time to work this out, bit by bit, there's no rush.

Ho passato il weekend a Roma – e wow, il tempo era fantastico.
(o pass-art-oh eel weekend a roam – er ay wow, eel tem-poe air-ah fan-tass-teek-oh)

You can now construct the sentence with which we started the chapter – and, as you will soon discover, this is just the very beginning of your journey into Italian!

Building Blocks

You just learnt how to say (amongst other things) "I spent the weekend in Rome – and wow, the weather was fantastic".

Now that you can do this, you are going to move on to expand what you can say through the use of additional "building blocks".

The new building blocks you are going to learn will allow you to begin instantly expanding your range of expressions in the Italian language.

So far, some of the building blocks you have already learnt include:

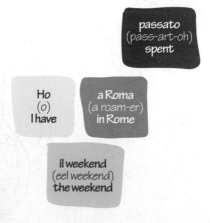

passato
(pass-art-oh)
spent

Ho
(o)
I have

a Roma
(a roam-er)
in Rome

il weekend
(eel weekend)
the weekend

You already know how to use these building blocks to construct a sentence. Once again, how would you say "I have spent the weekend in Rome"?

As you can see, you already know how to build the four building blocks above into a sentence. Take a look now at the six new building blocks below. Just have a glance over them and then I'll show you how you're going to add these into the mix of what you've learnt so far.

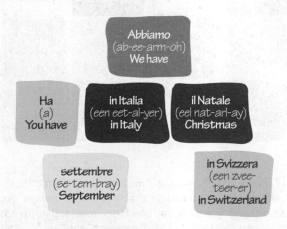

Okay, first things first: please don't to try to memorise them. No, no, no! Instead, I simply want you to play with your building blocks. After all, that's what building blocks are for, isn't it?

The way you're going to play with them is like this: on the next page, they have been put into four piles and all I want you to do is to make sentences with them. **You'll do this by using one building block from the first pile, one from the second, one from the third and one from the fourth.**

You will find that you can say a lot of different things using them in this way and it's up to you what sentences you make. The only thing I want you to make sure you do is to use every building block at least once. Also, please don't bother writing down the sentences you make. Instead, say them out loud. Or, if you're not in a place where you can do this, say them in your head. Now, off you go; make as many sentences as you can!

* Remember, of course, that "ho passato" means "I have spent", "I spent" and "I did spend". And this means, of course, that "ha passato" means "you have spent", "you spent" and "you did spend". And therefore "abbiamo passato" means not only "we have spent" but also "we spent" and "we did spend". Don't forget, you get three English past tenses for the price of one in Italian and this applies whether you're saying "I...", "you...", "we..." or whatever

The Checklist

You have now reached the final part of Chapter 1. Once you have finished this short section you will not only have completed your first chapter but you will also understand how this book works. All the other chapters follow the same pattern, with your Italian becoming ever more sophisticated as you complete each chapter.

The section you are now on will be the final part of each chapter and is what I call "The Checklist". It involves nothing more than a read-through of a selection of words or expressions you have so far encountered.

You will actually see The Checklist twice. The first time you will see that the Italian words are written in **black** (on the left-hand side) and that the English words are written in green (on the right-hand side) – and you know what green means... cover up!

So, what I want you to do here is to cover up the English words (which are written in green on the right-hand side) while you read through the list of Italian words on the left. Read through them all, from the top of the list to the bottom, and see if you can recall what they mean in English (uncover one green word at a time to check if you've remembered the meaning correctly). If you can go through the entire list, giving the correct English meaning for each of the Italian words / expressions **without making more than three mistakes in total**, then you're done. If not, then go through the list again. Keep doing this, either working from the top of the list to the bottom or from the bottom to the top (it doesn't matter which) until you can do it **without making more than three mistakes**.

Got it? Then let's go!

il weekend (eel weekend)	the weekend
romantico (roe-man-teek-oh)	romantic
fantastico (fan-tass-teek-oh)	fantastic
politico (pol-ee-teek-oh)	political
illogico (ee-lodge-eek-oh)	illogical
Ho (o)	I have
visitato (visit-art-oh)	visited
Ho visitato (o visit-art-oh)	I have visited / I visited / I did visit
Roma (roam-er)	Rome
Napoli (nap-oh-lee)	Naples

Ho visitato Napoli. (o visit-art-oh nap-oh-lee)	I have visited Naples / I visited Naples / I did visit Naples.
passato (pass-art-oh)	spent
Ho passato (o pass-art-oh)	I have spent / I spent / I did spend
Ha (a)	You have
Ha passato (a pass-art-oh)	You have spent / You spent / You did spend
Abbiamo (ab-ee-arm-oh)	We have
Abbiamo passato (ab-ee-arm-oh pass-art-oh)	We have spent / We spent / We did spend
settembre (se-tem-bray)	September
il Natale (eel nat-arl-ay)	Christmas
a Roma (a roam-er)	in Rome
in Italia (een eet-al-yer)	in Italy
in Svizzera (een zvee-tser-er)	in Switzerland
Abbiamo passato il Natale in Svizzera. (ab-ee-arm-oh pass-art-oh eel nat-arl-ay een zvee-tser-er)	We spent Christmas in Switzerland.
Ha passato settembre in Italia. (a pass-art-oh se-tem-bray een eet-al-yer)	You spent September in Italy.
e (ay)	and
Era (air-ah)	It was
Era fantastico. (air-ah fan-tass-teek-oh)	It was fantastic.
Il tempo era fantastico. (eel tem-poe air-ah fan-tass-teek-oh)	The weather was fantastic.
Ho passato il weekend a Roma – e wow, il tempo era fantastico. (o pass-art-oh eel weekend a roam-er ay wow, eel tem-poe air-ah fan-tass-teek-oh)	I spent the weekend in Rome – and wow, the weather was fantastic.

Finished working through that checklist and made fewer than three mistakes? Yes? Wonderful!

As that's the case, what I now want you to do is repeat exactly the same process with the checklist below, except that this time you'll be reading through the English and trying to recall the Italian. You'll be doing it the other way around. Just relax and work your way up and down the list until you can give the correct Italian translation for each of the *English* words / expressions **again without making more than three mistakes in total**. It's not a competition – and I'm not asking you to memorise them. Just look at the English words (on the left-hand side) while you cover up the green Italian words on the right-hand side and see if you can remember how to say them in Italian. You'll be surprised by how many you get right, even on the first try.

Okay, off you go!

the weekend	il weekend (eel weekend)
romantic	romantico (roe-man-teek-oh)
fantastic	fantastico (fan-tass-teek-oh)
political	politico (pol-ee-teek-oh)
illogical	illogico (ee-lodge-eek-oh)
I have	Ho (o)
visited	visitato (visit-art-oh)
I have visited / I visited / I did visit	Ho visitato (o visit-art-oh)
Rome	Roma (roam-er)
Naples	Napoli (nap-oh-lee)
I have visited Naples / I visited Naples / I did visit Naples.	Ho visitato Napoli. (o visit-art-oh nap-oh-lee)
spent	passato (pass-art-oh)
I have spent / I spent / I did spend	Ho passato (o pass-art-oh)
You have	Ha (a)
You have spent / You spent / You did spend	Ha passato (a pass-art-oh)
We have	Abbiamo (ab-ee-arm-oh)
We have spent / We spent / We did spend	Abbiamo passato (ab-ee-arm-oh pass-art-oh)
September	settembre (se-tem-bray)
Christmas	il Natale (eel nat-arl-ay)

in Rome	a Roma (a roam-er)
in Italy	in Italia (een eet-al-yer)
in Switzerland	in Svizzera (een zvee-tser-er)
We spent Christmas in Switzerland.	Abbiamo passato il Natale in Svizzera. (ab-ee-arm-oh pass-art-oh eel nat-arl-ay een zvee-tser-er)
You spent September in Italy.	Ha passato settembre in Italia. (a pass-art-oh se-tem-bray een eet-al-yer)
and	e (ay)
It was	Era (air-ah)
It was fantastic.	Era fantastico. (air-ah fan-tass-teek-oh)
The weather was fantastic.	Il tempo era fantastico. (eel-tem-poe air-ah fan-tass-teek-oh)
I spent the weekend in Rome – and wow, the weather was fantastic.	Ho passato il weekend a Roma – e wow, il tempo era fantastico. (o pass-art-oh eel weekend a roam-er ay wow, eel-tem-poe air-ah fan-tass-teek-oh)

Well, that's it, you're done with Chapter 1! Don't forget, you mustn't try to hold onto or remember anything you've learnt here. Anything you learn in earlier chapters will be brought up again and reinforced in later chapters. You don't need to do extra work or make any effort to memorise anything. The book has been organised to do that for you. Off you go and have a rest. You've earned it!

Between Chapters Tip!

Between chapters, I'm going to be giving you various tips on language learning. These will range from useful tips about the Italian language itself to advice on how to fit learning a language into your daily routine. Ready for the first one? Here it is!

Tip Number One – study (at least a little) every day!

Learning a language is like building a fire – if you don't tend to it, it will go out. So, once you have decided to learn a foreign language, you really should study it every day.

It doesn't have to be for a long time though. Just five or ten minutes each day will be enough, so long as you keep it up. Doing these five or ten minutes will stop you forgetting what you've already learnt and, over time, will let you put more meat on the bones of what you're learning.

As for what counts towards those five or ten minutes, well, that's up to you. Whilst you're working with this book, I would recommend that your five or ten minutes should be spent here, learning with me. Once you're done here, however, your daily study could be spent reading an Italian newspaper, watching an Italian film, or chatting with an Italian-speaking acquaintance. You could even attend a class if you want to learn in a more formal setting. The important thing is to make sure that you do a little every day.

CHAPTER 2

I booked a table, ordered dinner and then paid the bill.
What did you do?

> I booked a table, ordered dinner and then paid the bill. What did you do?

The first chapter has shown you that you can learn how to create full and complex sentences in Italian with relative ease. It also began to show you how to convert huge numbers of English words into Italian and then start using them straight away.

We will be doing more of both here, which will allow you to make enormous strides with your Italian in an incredibly short space of time.

Let's begin by carrying out a second Word Robbery...

Time to steal some words!
Word Robbery Number 2

The second group of words we are going to steal are words that end in "**ion**" and "**ation**". Words that end in "**ation**" in English usually end in "**azione**" in Italian. Take a look:

Words such as:

decoration	decorazione	domination	dominazione
cooperation	cooperazione	association	associazione
imagination	immaginazione	innovation	innovazione
preparation	preparazione	irritation	irritazione
donation	donazione		

There are more than 1250 "**ion**" words in English and they are related to similar words in Italian, as you can see above; we can start using these in Italian right now.

Adding them to the words we've already stolen so far, we have now reached a total of 2000 words stolen – and we're only on Chapter 2!

Words stolen so far 2000

We've now carried out our second Word Robbery and have gained more than a thousand words ending in "ion" and "ation", and it only took us thirty seconds to "learn" them.

Now, words ending "ation" in English actually come with yet another benefit. Not only can we steal them to use in Italian in the way shown above, but we can also utilise them to make the past tense in Italian.

Let me show you how.

Let's take "preparazione" (preparation) as an example.

Now, the first thing you're going to do with this "preparazione" is to cut off the "azione" at the end. Do this now – what are you left with?

prepar
(prep-are)

Good. Now, onto the end of this, I want you to add the "ato" from the end of the English word "tomato". So again, I simply want you to take "prepar" and add an "ato" onto the end of it.

What word does that give you?

preparato
(prep-are-art-oh)

This means "prepared".

Let's try doing this again, this time with the word "decorazione". Once more, cut off the "azione" from the end of the word and replace it with the "ato" you find at the end of the English word "tomato".

Doing this, what do you get?

decorato
(deck-or-art-oh)

This means "decorated".

Now, you will find that there is always an exception to any rule and, in this, an important exception is the word "reservation". Italians do not like to make reservations as we do, instead an Italian will make a "prenotation" with the idea being that someone will pre-note the thing they want – a table, a room, and so on – rather than reserve it.

So, given that English words ending in "ation" end in "azione" in Italian, how do you think you would say "reservation" (literally "prenotation") in Italian?

prenotazione
(pray-no-tatz-ee-oh-nay)

And now that we know what "reservation" is in Italian, we can once again cut the "azione" from the end and add the "ato" from "tomato" in its place. This will give us the Italian for "reserved" (literally "pre-noted"). So, cut off the "azione" from "prenotazione", replace it with "ato" and tell me what "reserved" or "pre-noted" is in Italian:

prenotato
(pray-no-tart-oh)

Now again, what is "I have" in Italian?

Ho
(o)

So, how would you say "I have reserved" (literally "I have pre-noted")?

Ho prenotato
(o pray-no-tart-oh)

And "I reserved" / "I pre-noted"?

Ho prenotato
(o pray-no-tart-oh)

And "I did reserve" / "I did pre-note"?

Ho prenotato
(o pray-no-tart-oh)

(Once again, just in case you'd forgotten, you get three English past tenses for the price of one in Italian!)

Now again, how would you say "prepared" in Italian?

preparato
(prep-are-art-oh)

How would you say "I have prepared"?

Ho preparato
(o prep-are-art-oh)

And "I prepared"?

Ho preparato
(o prep-are-art-oh)

And "I did prepare"?

Ho preparato
(o prep-are-art-oh)

"The dinner" in Italian is:

la cena
(la chain-er)

So, how would you say "I have prepared the dinner", "I prepared the dinner", "I did prepare the dinner"?

Ho preparato la cena.
(o prep-are-art-oh la chain-er)

And again, what is "reserved" (literally "pre-noted") in Italian?

prenotato
(pray-no-tart-oh)

Italians actually use this word to mean both
"reserved" and "booked". So, how would you say,
"I have reserved" / "I have booked" / "I have
pre-noted"?

Ho prenotato
(o pray-no-tart-oh)

"A table" in Italian is:

un tavolo
(oon tav-oh-loe)

So, how would you say "I have reserved a table" / "I have booked a table"?

Ho prenotato un tavolo.
(o pray-no-tart-oh oon tav-oh-loe)

"For you" in Italian is:

per Lei
(pair lay)

How would you say "I have reserved a table for you" / "I have booked a table
for you"?

Ho prenotato un tavolo per Lei.
(o pray-no-tart-oh oon tav-oh-loe pair lay)

And again, what was "the dinner" in Italian?

la cena
(la chain-er)

And what was "for you"?

per Lei
(pair lay)

So, if "per Lei" means "for you", what do you think is the word for "for" in Italian?

per
(pair)

Now, to say "for dinner" in Italian, you will literally say "for the dinner". How do you think you would say that?

per la cena
(pair la chain-er)

Alright, how would you say "I have reserved a table for dinner" / "I have booked a table for dinner"?

Ho prenotato un tavolo per la cena.
(o pray-no-tart-oh oon tav-oh-loe pair la chain-er)

So, as you can see, those "ation" / "azione" words we stole at the beginning of this chapter really are very useful. Not only do they give you a way to begin to access more than a thousand words immediately – words like "preparation" (preparazione), "decoration" (decorazione), "cooperation" (cooperazione), and so on – but these "ation" words also give you access to the past tense in Italian. This is because, by simply cutting off the "ation" / "azione" from the end of the word and then adding the "ato" from "tomato" in its place, you can create hundreds of past tense words in Italian; words such as "preparato" (prepared), "decorato" (decorated) or, in a more unusual example, "prenotato" (pre-noted), meaning "reserved".

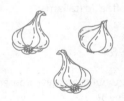

Let's try another somewhat unusual one now.

What would "ordination" be in Italian?

ordinazione
(or-din-atz-ee-oh-nay)

And so, cutting off the "azione" and replacing it with the "ato" from "tomato", what would "ordained" be in Italian?

ordinato
(or-din-art-oh)

Now, you are probably asking yourself "why on earth am I being taught the words for 'ordination' and 'ordained'?"

Well, the word "ordination" / "ordinazione" refers to "the granting of holy orders" and, even more literally, means something simpler still like "ordering".

When you cut off the "ation" / "azione" from the end of it and add the "ato" from tomato in its place, you end up with the Italian word that means "ordered".

Now that you know this, how would you say in Italian "I have ordered", "I ordered", "I did order"?

Ho ordinato
(o or-din-art-oh)

And how would you say "I ordered dinner" (you will say literally "I *have* ordered *the* dinner")?

Ho ordinato la cena.
(o or-din-art-oh la chain-er)

"The coffee" in Italian is:

il caffè
(eel ka-fe)

So how would you say "I ordered coffee" (again, you will literally say "I *have* ordered *the* coffee")?

Ho ordinato il caffè.
(o or-din-art-oh eel ka-fe)

And once again, how would you say "for you"?

per Lei
(pair lay)

And so how would you say "I ordered the coffee for you"?

Ho ordinato il caffè per Lei.
(o or-din-art-oh eel ka-fe pair lay)

Good, now can you recall how to say "I visited"?

Ho visitato
(o visit-art-oh)

How about "I spent"?

Ho passato
(o pass-art-oh)

"I reserved" / "I booked"?

Ho prenotato
(o pray-no-tart-oh)

"I prepared"?

Ho preparato
(o prep-are-art-oh)

"I ordered"?

Ho ordinato
(o or-din-art-oh)

"Paid" in Italian is:

pagato
(pag-art-oh)

So, how would you say "I have paid", "I paid", "I did pay"?

Ho pagato
(o pag-art-oh)

Do you remember what "we have" is from the "Building Blocks" section in Chapter 1?
If not, don't worry, it's:

Abbiamo
(ab-ee-arm-oh)

So, with this in mind, how would you say "we have paid", "we paid", "we did pay"?

Abbiamo pagato
(ab-ee-arm-oh pag-art-oh)

And do you remember what "you have" is in Italian?

Ha
(a)

So, how would you say "you have paid"?

Ha pagato
(a pag-art-oh)

"The bill" in Italian is literally "the account", which is:

il conto
(eel kon-toe)

So, how would you say "you have paid the bill"?

Ha pagato il conto.
(a pag-art-oh eel kon-toe)

How about "we have paid the bill"?

Abbiamo pagato il conto.
(ab-ee-arm-oh pag-art-oh eel kon-toe)

And "I have paid the bill"?

Ho pagato il conto.
(o pag-art-oh eel kon-toe)

Again, how would you say "I booked a table"?

Ho prenotato un tavolo.
(o pray-no-tart-oh oon tav-oh-loe)

What about "I ordered the dinner"?

Ho ordinato la cena.
(o or-din-art-oh la chain-er)

And how about "I paid the bill"?

Ho pagato il conto.
(o pag-art-oh eel kon-toe)

Let's now try making a list out of these things. Start by saying "I booked a table, ordered the dinner, paid the bill." Take your time working it out in your head, bit by bit – there really is no rush. So again "I booked a table, ordered the dinner, paid the bill":

Ho prenotato un tavolo, ordinato la cena, pagato il conto.
(o pray-no-tart-oh oon tav-oh-loe, or-din-art-oh la chain-er, pag-art-oh eel kon-toe)

Let's add "then" into this sentence to make it sound more natural. "Then" in Italian is:

poi
(poy)

First try simply saying "then paid the bill". How would you say that?

poi pagato il conto
(poy pag-art-oh eel kon-toe)

And what was "and" in Italian?

e
(ay)

Right, now say "and then paid the bill".

e poi pagato il conto
(ey poy pag-art-oh eel kon-toe)

Okay. Let's try to put this all together and say "I booked a table, ordered the dinner and then paid the bill."

Ho prenotato un tavolo, ordinato la cena e poi pagato il conto.
(o pray-no-tart-oh oon tav-oh-loe, or-din-art-oh la chain-er ey poy pag-art-oh eel kon-toe)

Not a bad sentence. Let's make it bigger still.
What is "you have" in Italian?

Ha
(a)

And what is "prepared"?

preparato
(prep-are-art-oh)

So, how would you say "you have prepared"?

Ha preparato
(a prep-are-art-oh)

If you want to say "what have you prepared?" in Italian, one very typical way to express this is to literally say "*what thing* you have prepared?"

"What thing" in Italian is:

Che cosa
(ke koe-ser)

Again, how would you say "you have prepared" in Italian?

Ha preparato
(a prep-are-art-oh)

And how would you say "what thing"?

Che cosa
(ke koe-ser)

46

To say "what have you prepared?", you can simply say "what thing you have prepared?" Let's do that now. Again, what is "what thing"?

Che cosa
(ke koe-ser)

And what is "you have prepared"?

Ha preparato
(a prep-are-art-oh)

So, how would you say "what thing you have prepared?"?

Che cosa ha preparato?
(ke koe-ser a prep-are-art-oh)

Literally this means "what thing you have prepared?", but it means not only "what have you prepared?", it also means "what did you prepare?"
Just as before, even though it's a question, you still get more than one English past tense for the price of one in Italian.

Let's just make sure you've understood this 100%. How would you say "what have you prepared?"?

Che cosa ha preparato?
(ke koe-ser a prep-are-art-oh)

And "what did you prepare"?

Che cosa ha preparato?
(ke koe-ser a prep-are-art-oh)

So, they're the same!

And how do you think would you say "what have you reserved?" / "what did you reserve?" (literally "what thing you have reserved (pre-noted))"?

Che cosa ha prenotato?
(ke koe-ser a pray-no-tart-oh)

The word for "done" in Italian is:

fatto
(fat-oh)

So, how would you say "what have you done?" / "what did you do?" (literally "what thing you have done?")?

Che cosa ha fatto?
(ke koe-ser a fat-oh)

And once more, how would you say "I reserved a table" / "I booked a table"?

Ho prenotato un tavolo.
(o pray-no-tart-oh oon tav-oh-loe)

And how would you say "I ordered the dinner"?

Ho ordinato la cena.
(o or-din-art-oh la chain-er)

And remind me, what was the word for "then" in Italian?

poi
(poy)

And the word for "and"?

e
(ay)

So, now say "and then paid the bill".

e poi pagato il conto
(ey poy pag-art-oh eel kon-toe)

Let's put those bits together again and say "I booked a table, ordered the dinner and then paid the bill."

Ho prenotato un tavolo, ordinato la cena e poi pagato il conto.
(o pray-no-tart-oh oon tav-oh-loe, or-din-art-oh la chain-er ey poy pag-art-oh eel kon-toe)

And let's add the final bit onto it all. Again, how would you say "what thing?"

Che cosa
(ke koe-ser)

And, as I mentioned earlier, "you have done" in Italian is:

Ha fatto
(a fat-oh)

So, how would you say "what have you done?" / "what did you do?" (literally "what thing you have done?") ?

Che cosa ha fatto?
(ke koe-ser a fat-oh)

Now let's combine absolutely everything together and (taking your time to think it out) say "I booked a table, ordered dinner and then paid the bill. What did you do?".

Ho prenotato un tavolo, ordinato la cena e poi pagato il conto. Che cosa ha fatto?
(o pray-no-tart-oh oon tav-oh-loe, or-din-art-oh la chain-er, ey poy pag-art-oh eel kon-toe. ke koe-ser a fat-oh)

How did you find that final, complex sentence? Try it a few more times, even if you got it right, until you feel comfortable constructing it. Every time you practise building these long sentences, the naturalness and fluidity of your spoken Italian will improve and your confidence in speaking will get better along with it.

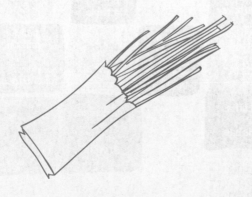

Building Blocks 2

It's time to add some new building blocks to the mix. As before, it will be just six new ones. Here they are:

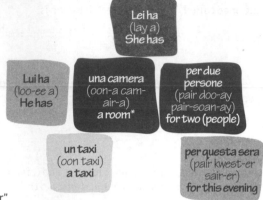

* literally "a chamber"

Once more, these new building blocks have been put into four piles below. As previously, what I want you to do is to make sentences with them, each time using one building block from the first pile, one from the second, one from the third and one from the fourth. Make as many sentences as you can!

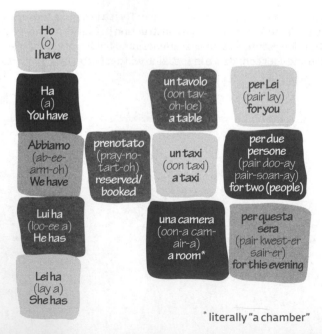

* literally "a chamber"

You have now reached your second checklist. Remember, don't skip anything! The checklists are essential if you want what you've learnt to remain in your memory for the long term.

So again, cover up the English words on the right-hand side while you read through the list of Italian words on the left, trying to recall what they mean in English. If you can go through the entire list, giving the correct English meaning for each of the Italian words / expressions **without making more than three mistakes in total**, then you're done. If not, then go through the list again. Keep doing this, either working from the top of the list to the bottom or from the bottom to the top (it doesn't matter which) until you can do it **without making more than three mistakes**.

Okay. Ready, set, go!

il weekend (eel weekend)	the weekend
romantico (roe-man-teek-oh)	romantic
fantastico (fan-tass-teek-oh)	fantastic
politico (pol-ee-teek-oh)	political
illogico (ee-lodge-eek-oh)	illogical
Ho (o)	I have
visitato (visit-art-oh)	visited
Ho visitato (o visit-art-oh)	I have visited / I visited / I did visit
Roma (roam-er)	Rome
Napoli (nap-oh-lee)	Naples
Ho visitato Napoli. (o visit-art-oh nap-oh-lee)	I have visited Naples / I visited Naples / I did visit Naples.
passato (pass-art-oh)	spent
Ho passato (o pass-art-oh)	I have spent / I spent / I did spend
Ha (a)	You have
Ha passato (a pass-art-oh)	You have spent / You spent / You did spend
Abbiamo (ab-ee-arm-oh)	We have

Abbiamo passato (ab-ee-arm-oh pass-art-oh)	We have spent / We spent / We did spend
settembre (se-tem-bray)	September
il Natale (eel nat-arl-ay)	Christmas
a Roma (a roam-er)	in Rome
in Italia (een eet-al-yer)	in Italy
in Svizzera (een zvee-tser-er)	in Switzerland
Abbiamo passato il Natale in Svizzera. (ab-ee-arm-oh pass-art-oh eel nat-arl-ay een zvee-tser-er)	We have spent Christmas in Switzerland / We spent Christmas in Switzerland / We did spend Christmas in Switzerland.
Ha passato settembre in Italia. (a pass-art-oh se-tem-bray een eet-al-yer)	You have spent September in Italy / You spent September in Italy / You did spend September in Italy.
e (ay)	and
Era (air-ah)	It was
Era fantastico. (air-ah fan-tass-teek-oh)	It was fantastic.
Il tempo era fantastico. (eel-tem-poe air-ah fan-tass-teek-oh)	The weather was fantastic.
Ho passato il weekend a Roma – e wow, il tempo era fantastico. (o pass-art-oh eel weekend a roam-er ay wow, eel-tem-poe air-ah fan-tass-teek-oh)	I spent the weekend in Rome – and wow, the weather was fantastic.
preparazione (prep-are-atz-ee-oh-nay)	preparation
preparato (pray-par-ato)	prepared
prenotazione (pray-no-tatz-ee-oh-nay)	reservation
prenotato (pray-no-tart-oh)	reserved / booked
ordinato (or-din-art-oh)	ordered
pagato (pag-art-oh)	paid
fatto (fat-oh)	done

il conto (eel kon-toe)	the bill
la cena (la chain-er)	the dinner
il caffè (eel ka-fe)	the coffee
un tavolo (oon tav-oh-loe)	a table
una camera (oon a cam-air-a)	a room
un taxi (oon taxi)	a taxi
Ho preparato la cena. (o prep-are-art-oh la chain-er)	I have prepared the dinner / I prepared the dinner / I did prepare the dinner.
Ho ordinato il caffè per la cena. (o or-din-art-oh eel ka-fe pair la chain-er)	I have ordered coffee for dinner / I ordered coffee for dinner / I did order coffee for dinner.
Ho prenotato un tavolo per Lei. (o pray-no-tart-oh oon tav-oh-loe pair lay)	I have booked a table for you / I booked a table for you / I did book a table for you.
Lei ha (lay a)	She has
Lei ha prenotato un tavolo per questa sera. (lay a pray-no-tart-oh oon tav-oh-loe pair kwest-er sair-er)	She has booked / reserved a table for this evening – She booked / reserved a table for this evening – She did book / reserve a table for this evening.
Lui ha (loo-ee a)	He has
Lui ha prenotato una camera per due persone. (loo-ee a pray-no-tart-oh oon-a cam-air-a pair doo-ay pair-soan-ay)	He has booked / reserved a room for two people – He booked / reserved a room for two people – He did book / reserve a room for two people.
Abbiamo prenotato un taxi per Lei. (ab-ee-arm-oh pray-no-tart-oh oon taxi pair lay)	We have booked a taxi for you / We booked a taxi for you / We did book a taxi for you.
Abbiamo pagato il conto. (ab-ee-arm-oh pag-art-oh eel kon-toe)	We paid the bill / We have paid the the bill / We did pay the bill.
Che cosa? (ke koe-ser)	What? / What thing?
Che cosa ha preparato? (ke koe-ser a prep-are-art-oh)	What have you prepared? / What did you prepare? (literally "What thing you have prepared?")

Che cosa ha fatto? (ke koe-ser a fat-oh)	What have you done? / What did you do? (literally "What thing you have done?")
Ho prenotato un tavolo, ordinato la cena e poi pagato il conto. Che cosa ha fatto? (o pray-no-tart-oh oon tav-oh-loe, or-din-art-oh la chain-er ey poy pag-art-oh eel kon-toe. ke koe-ser a fat-oh)	I booked a table, ordered dinner and then paid the bill. What did you do?

Now, do the same thing once again below, except that this time you'll be reading through the list of English words and trying to recall the Italian. All you need to do is to be able to do one full read-through of them without making more than three mistakes in total and you're done!

the weekend	**il weekend** (eel weekend)
romantic	**romantico** (roe-man-teek-oh)
fantastic	**fantastico** (fan-tass-teek-oh)
political	**politico** (pol-ee-teek-oh)
illogical	**illogico** (ee-lodge-eek-oh)
I have	**Ho** (o)
visited	**visitato** (visit-art-oh)
I have visited / I visited / I did visit	**Ho visitato** (o visit-art-oh)
Rome	**Roma** (roam-er)
Naples	**Napoli** (nap-oh-lee)
I have visited Naples / I visited Naples / I did visit Naples.	**Ho visitato Napoli.** (o visit-art-oh nap-oh-lee)
spent	**passato** (pass-art-oh)
I have spent / I spent / I did spend	**Ho passato** (o pass-art-oh)
You have	**Ha** (a)
You have spent / You spent / You did spend	**Ha passato** (a pass-art-oh)
We have	**Abbiamo** (ab-ee-arm-oh)
We have spent / We spent / We did spend	**Abbiamo passato** (ab-ee-arm-oh pass-art-oh)

September	settembre (se-tem-bray)
Christmas	il Natale (eel nat-arl-ay)
in Rome	a Roma (a roam-er)
in Italy	in Italia (een eet-al-yer)
In Switzerland	in Svizzera (een zvee-tser-er)
We have spent Christmas in Switzerland / We spent Christmas in Switzerland / We did spend Christmas in Switzerland.	Abbiamo passato il Natale in Svizzera. (ab-ee-arm-oh pass-art-oh eel nat-arl-ay een zvee-tser-er)
You have spent September in Italy / You spent September in Italy / You did spend September in Italy.	Ha passato settembre in Italia. (a pass-art-oh se-tem-bray een eet-al-yer)
and	e (ay)
It was	Era (air-ah)
It was fantastic.	Era fantastico. (air-ah fan-tass-teek-oh)
The weather was fantastic.	Il tempo era fantastico. (eel-tem-poe air-ah fan-tass-teek-oh)
I spent the weekend in Rome – and wow, the weather was fantastic.	Ho passato il weekend a Roma – e wow, il tempo era fantastico. (o pass-art-oh eel weekend a roam-er ay wow, eel-tem-poe air-ah fan-tass-teek-oh)
preparation	preparazione (prep-are-atz-ee-oh-nay)
prepared	preparato (pray-par-ay)
reservation	prenotazione (pray-no-tatz-ee-oh-nay)
reserved / booked	prenotato (pray-no-tart-oh)
ordered	ordinato (or-din-art-oh)
paid	pagato (pag-art-oh)
done	fatto (fat-oh)
the bill	il conto (eel kon-toe)
the dinner	la cena (la chain-er)
the coffee	il caffè (eel ka-fe)

a table	**un tavolo** (oon tav-oh-loe)
a room	**una camera** (oon-a cam-air-a)
a taxi	**un taxi** (oon taxi)
I have prepared the dinner / I prepared the dinner / I did prepare the dinner.	**Ho preparato la cena.** (o prep-are-art-oh la chain-er)
I have ordered coffee for dinner / I ordered coffee for dinner / I did order coffee for dinner.	**Ho ordinato il caffè per la cena.** (o or-din-art-oh eel ka-fe pair la chain-er)
I have booked a table for you / I booked a table for you / I did book a table for you.	**Ho prenotato un tavolo per Lei.** (o pray-no-tart-oh oon tav-oh-loe pair lay)
She has	**Lei ha** (lay a)
She has booked / reserved a table for this evening – She booked / reserved a table for this evening – She did book / reserve a table for this evening.	**Lei ha prenotato un tavolo per questa sera.** (lay a pray-no-tart-oh oon tav-oh-loe pair kwest-er sair-er)
He has	**Lui ha** (loo-ee a)
He has booked / reserved a room for two people – He booked / reserved a room for two people – He did book / reserve a room for two people.	**Lui ha prenotato una camera per due persone.** (loo-ee a pray-no-tart-oh oon-a cam-air-a pair doo-ay pair-soan-ay)
We have booked a taxi for you / We booked a taxi for you / We did book a taxi for you.	**Abbiamo prenotato un taxi per Lei.** (ab-ee-arm-oh pray-no-tart-oh oon taxi pair lay)
We paid the bill / We have paid the bill / We did pay the bill.	**Abbiamo pagato il conto.** (ab-ee-arm-oh pag-art-oh eel kon-toe)
What? / What thing?	**Che cosa?** (ke koe-ser)
What have you prepared? / What did you prepare? (literally "What thing you have prepared?")	**Che cosa ha preparato?** (ke koe-ser a prep-are-art-oh)
What have you done? / What did you do? (literally "What thing you have done?")	**Che cosa ha fatto?** (ke koe-ser a fat-oh)

I booked a table, ordered dinner and then paid the bill. What did you do?

Ho prenotato un tavolo, ordinato la cena e poi pagato il conto. Che cosa ha fatto? (o pray-no-tart-oh oon tav-oh-loe, or-din-art-oh la chain-er ey poy pag-art-oh eel kon-toe. ke koe-ser a fat-oh)

Well, that's it, you're done with Chapter 2! Remember, don't try to hold onto anything you've learnt here. Everything you learn in earlier chapters will be brought back up and reinforced in later chapters. You don't need to do anything or make any effort to memorise words. The book has been organised in such a way that it will do that for you. Off you go now and have a rest, please!

Stop while you're still enjoying it!

Arnold Schwarzenegger once said that the key to his bodybuilding success was that he stopped his workout each day just before it started to get boring. On the few occasions he went past that point, he found it incredibly hard to return to the gym again the next day – and he *loved* working out.

As you will almost certainly recall, Tip 1 suggested that you should study every day – which you definitely should do if you can. But that doesn't mean that you should overdo it. So, if you're not really in the mood, just do five minutes. If you are in the mood though, don't push yourself too hard. Stop before you get to the point where it doesn't feel fun any longer. Best to leave yourself feeling hungry for more rather than bloated and fed up!

CHAPTER 3

I'm scared of flying, so I'm planning to take the Eurostar.

> I'm scared of flying, so I'm planning to take the Eurostar.

Person 1:	I'm planning to go back to Italy in May.
Person 2:	Really?
Person 1:	Yes, I feel like going back to Rome but I'm scared of flying, so I'm planning to take the Eurostar.

The brief conversation above does not seem complicated in English and yet, even if you have studied Italian before, you might well find it impossible to know exactly where to begin in order to say all of this in Italian. By the end of this chapter, you will have learnt how to carry out both sides of this conversation, plus a great deal of other Italian words and expressions besides.

Let's begin!

Again, what is "I have" in Italian?

Ho
(*o*)

And how would you say "I have visited", "I visited", "I did visit"?

Ho visitato
(*o visit-art-oh*)

"I have spent", "I spent", "I did spend"?

Ho passato
(*o pass-art-oh*)

"I have reserved", "I reserved", "I did reserve"?

Ho prenotato
(o pray-no-tart-oh)

"I have ordered", "I ordered", "I did order"?

Ho ordinato
(o or-din-art-oh)

"I have prepared", "I prepared", "I did prepare"?

Ho preparato
(o prep-are-art-oh)

"I have paid", "I paid", I did pay"?

Ho pagato
(o pag-art-oh)

"I have done", "I did", "I did do"?

Ho fatto
(o fat-oh)

So, you definitely know how to use "I have" in Italian to express a number of things in the past tense.

However, "I have" is not only useful for talking about things that have happened in the past. It also opens up a wide range of extremely useful expressions in Italian that allow you, for example, to talk about what you're planning to do, feel like doing, or can't stand doing. This is really useful everyday language that will help your Italian sound natural and colloquial.

Let's start building towards using these expressions now.

To say "to reserve", "to book" or, more literally, "to pre-note" in Italian, you can once again create this word out of the Italian word for "reservation" (literally "prenotation").

So remind me, what was "reservation" ("prenotation") in Italian?

prenotazione
(pray-no-tatz-ee-oh-nay)

Now, if you want to say "to reserve" or "to book", you will once again cut the "azione" off the end of "prenotazione" but this time you're going to replace it with "are" (pronounced "are-ray").

So, do that now, cut the "azione" off the end of "prenotazione" and add "are" in its place. What do you get?

prenotare
(pray-no-tar-ray)

This means "to reserve" or "to book".

Now, what is "a table" in Italian?

un tavolo
(oon tav-oh-loe)

So, how would you say "to reserve / to book a table"?

prenotare un tavolo
(pray-no-tar-ray oon tav-oh-loe)

And again, what is "I have" in Italian?

Ho
(o)

"Intention" in Italian is:

intenzione
(in-ten-tzee-oh-nay)

Alright, how would you say "I have intention"?

Ho intenzione
(o lon-ton-syon)

The word for "of" in Italian is:

di
(dee)

So, how would you say "I have intention of"?

Ho intenzione di
(o in-ten-tzee-oh-nay dee)

Saying "I have intention of…" is actually one way of saying "I'm planning to…" in Italian.

With this in mind, how would you say "I'm planning to book a table" / "I'm planning to reserve a table" (literally "I have intention of to reserve a table")?

Ho intenzione di prenotare un tavolo.
(o in-ten-tzee-oh-nay dee pray-no-tar-ray oon tav-oh-loe)

Okay, once more, what was "for this evening" in Italian?

per questa sera
(pair kwest-er sair-er)

Now, how would you say "I'm planning to book a table for this evening" / "I'm planning to reserve a table for this evening" (literally "I have intention of to reserve a table for this evening")?

Ho intenzione di prenotare un tavolo per questa sera.
(o in-ten-tzee-oh-nay dee pray-no-tar-ray oon tav-oh-loe pair kwest-er sair-er)

And what was "a room" in Italian?

una camera
(oon-a cam-air-a)

How would you say "I'm planning to book a room for this evening"?

Ho intenzione di prenotare una camera per questa sera.
(o in-ten-tzee-oh-nay dee pray-no-tar-ray oon-a cam-air-a pair kwest-er sair-er)

"To go back" in Italian is literally "to return", which in Italian is:

ritornare
(ree-torn-are-ay)

So, how would you say "I'm planning to go back"?

Ho intenzione di ritornare.
(o in-ten-tzee-oh-nay dee ree-torn-are-ay)

And again, how would you say "in Italy"?

in Italia (een eet-al-yer)

"To Italy" is said in *exactly the same way* as "in Italy". Try it! How would you say "to Italy"?

in Italia (een eet-al-yer)

And how would you say "I'm planning to go back (literally "to return") to Italy"?

Ho intenzione di ritornare in Italia.
(o In-ten-tzee-oh-nay dee ri-torn-are-ay een eet-al-yer)

"In May" in Italian is:

a maggio
(a madge-oh)

With this in mind, how would you say "I'm planning to go back to Italy in May"?

Ho intenzione di ritornare in Italia a maggio.
(o in-ten-tzee-oh-nay dee ri-torn-are-ay een eet-al-yer a madge-oh)

To recap, in Italian, if you want to say "I'm planning to..." you can simply use "I have intention of...".

It's an extremely useful expression and actually is just one of a number of such expressions that work in more or less the same way.

For example, if you want to say "I feel like…" or "I fancy…" in Italian, you will literally say "I have want of…" which in Italian is:

Ho voglia di
(o vol-ya dee)

Knowing this, how would you say "I feel like going back to Italy in May / I fancy going back to Italy in May" (literally "I have want of to return to Italy in May")?

Ho voglia di ritornare in Italia a maggio.
(o vol-ya dee ri-torn-are-ay een eet-al-yer a madge-oh)

What is "September" in Italian?

settembre
(se-tem-bray)

So, how would you say "in September"?

a settembre
(a se-tem-bray)

And how would you say "I feel like going back to Italy in September / I fancy going back to Italy in September" (literally "I have want of to return to Italy in September")?

Ho voglia di ritornare in Italia a settembre.
(o vol-ya dee ri-torn-are-ay een eet-al-yer a se-tem-bray)

Do you remember how to say "in Rome"?

a Roma
(a roam-er)

"To Rome" in Italian is said in exactly the same way – how would you say "to Rome"?

a Roma
(a roam-er)

And how would you say "I feel like going back to Rome / I fancy going back to Rome"?

Ho voglia di ritornare a Roma.
(o vol-ya dee ri-torn-are-ay a roam-er)

You have now practised using two phrases that are constructed in a similar way. The first uses the words "I have intention of…" to express "I'm planning to…" and the other uses the words "I have want of…" to mean "I feel like…" or "I fancy…".

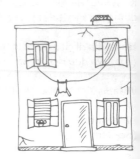

Let's add another one to the mix. But again, don't worry about trying to memorise any of this. As you work your way through the rest of the chapter, you'll find that everything comes up again and again, jolting your memory each time and helping those words and phrases to stick without you having to resort to memorising or learning by rote. You will be reminded of these things when the time is right.

Now, to say "I'm scared of…" in Italian, you will literally say "I have fear of…", which is:

Ho paura di…
(o pow-oo-rer dee)

So, how would you say "I'm scared of going back to Rome" (literally "I have fear of to return to Rome")?

Ho paura di ritornare a Roma.
(o pow-oo-rer dee ri-torn-are-ay a roam-er)

How about "I'm scared of going back to Italy"?

Ho paura di ritornare in Italia.
(o pow-oo-rer dee ri-torn-are-ay een eet-al-yer)

And "I'm scared of going back to Italy in September"?

Ho paura di ritornare in Italia a settembre.
(o pow-oo-rer dee ri-torn-are-ay een eet-al-yer a se-tem-bray)

"To fly" or "flying" in Italian is:

volare
(vol-are-ay)

How would you say "I'm scared of flying"?

Ho paura di volare.
(o pow-oo-rer dee vol-are-ay)

The word for "but" in Italian is:

ma
(mu)

Right, how would you say "...but I'm scared of flying" (literally "...but I have fear of flying")?

...ma ho paura di volare
(mu o pow-oo-rer dee vol-are-ay)

And again, how would you say "I feel like going back to Rome / I fancy going back to Rome" (literally "I have want of to return to Rome")?

Ho voglia di ritornare a Roma.
(o vol-ya dee ri-torn-are-ay a roam-er)

Let's put those bits together now and say "I feel like going back to Rome but I'm scared of flying":

Ho voglia di ritornare a Roma ma ho paura di volare.
(o vol-ya dee ri-torn-are-ay a roam-er mu o pow-oo-rer dee vol-are-ay)

Good. So again, how would you say "I feel like... / I fancy... / I have want of..."?

Ho voglia di...
(o vol-ya dee)

And how would you say "I'm scared of... / I have fear of..."?

Ho paura di...
(o pow-oo-rer dee)

And can you remember how to say "I'm planning to… / I have intention of…"?

Ho intenzione di…
(o in-ten-tzee-oh-nay dee)

"To take" in Italian is:

prendere
(pren-de-rey)

And "the Eurostar" in Italian is quite simply:

l'Eurostar
(lay-oo-roe-star)

How would you say "to take the Eurostar"?

prendere l'Eurostar
(pren-de-rey lay-oo-roe-star)

Next, how would you say "I'm planning to take the Eurostar"?

Ho intenzione di prendere l'Eurostar.
(o in-ten-tzee-oh-nay dee pren-de-rey lay-oo-roe-star)

"So" in Italian is:

quindi
(kwin-dee)

With this in mind, how would you say "…so I'm planning to take the Eurostar"?

…quindi ho intenzione di prendere l'Eurostar.
(kwin-dee o in-ten-tzee-oh-nay dee pren-de-rey lay-oo-roe-star)

And again, how would you say "I'm frightened of…"?

Ho paura di…
(o pow-oo-rer dee)

And "I'm frightened of flying"?

Ho paura di volare.
(o pow-oo-rer dee vol-are-ay)

Knowing this, how would you say "I'm frightened of flying, so I'm planning to take the Eurostar"?

Ho paura di volare, quindi ho intenzione di prendere l'Eurostar.
(o pow-oo-rer dee vol-are-ay, kwin-dee o in-ten-tzee-oh-nay dee pren-de-rey lay-oo-roe-star)

And once more, how would you say "I feel like… / I fancy…" in Italian?

Ho voglia di…
(o vol-ya dee)

Extend this now, saying "I feel like going back to Rome":

Ho voglia di ritornare a Roma.
(o vol-ya dee ri-torn-are-ay a roam-er)

And remind me, what is "but" in Italian?

ma
(mu)

Now, how would you say "I feel like going back to Rome but I'm scared of flying, so I'm planning to take the Eurostar"? Take your time with this sentence, building it slowly, bit by bit, and think out each part as you work through it. If you feel it's too much of a struggle, feel free to take a break and to go over the beginning of the chapter again. There really is no rush.

Give it a go, how would you say "I feel like going back to Rome but I'm scared of flying, so I'm planning to take the Eurostar"?

Ho voglia di ritornare a Roma ma ho paura di volare, quindi ho intenzione di prendere l'Eurostar.
(o vol-ya dee ri-torn-are-ay a roam-er mu o pow-oo-rer dee vol-are-ay, kwin-dee o in-ten-tzee-oh-nay dee pren-de-rey lay-oo-roe-star)

It's a long and complex sentence, so feel free to go through it a few times even once you do get it right.

Okay, let's try putting this together with the rest of the dialogue from the beginning of the chapter. You already know almost everything you need for it.

Start by being Person 1 from the dialogue and say "I feel like going back to Italy in May":

Ho voglia di ritornare in Italia a maggio.
(o vol-ya dee ri-torn-are-ay een eet-al-yer a madge-oh)

Person 2 is now going to reply to this simply by saying "really?" "Really" in Italian is:

veramente
(ve-ra-men-tay)

Reply to that earlier statement saying simply "really?":

Veramente?
(ve-ra-men-tay)

"Yes" in Italian is:

sì
(see)

You reply to Person 2, saying "Yes, I feel like going back to Rome but I'm scared of flying, so I'm planning to take the Eurostar." How will you say that? Again, take your time:

Sì, ho voglia di ritornare a Roma ma ho paura di volare, quindi ho intenzione di prendere l'Eurostar.
(see, o vol-ya dee ri-torn-are-ay a roam-er mu o pow-oo-rer dee vol-are-ay, kwin-dee o in-ten-tzee-oh-nay dee pren-de-rey lay-oo-roe-star)

Good. Now, with that done, try going through the entire dialogue all in one go:

I'm planning to go back to Italy in May.
Ho *voglia di ritornare in Italia a maggio.*
(*o vol-ya dee ri-torn-are-ay een eet-al-yer a madge-oh*)

Really?
Veramente?
(*ve-ra-men-tay*)

Yes, I feel like going back to Rome but I'm scared of flying, so I'm planning to take the Eurostar.
Sì, ho voglia di ritornare a Roma ma ho paura di volare, quindi ho intenzione di prendere l'Eurostar.
(*see, o vol-ya dee ri-torn-are-ay a roam-er mu o pow-oo-rer dee vol-are-ay, kwin-dee o in-ten-tzee-oh-nay dee pren-de-rey lay-oo-roe-star*)

That was an extremely complex dialogue which contained a lot of different ideas and phrases that needed to be juggled. If you felt unclear regarding how to construct any of the different parts it was made up of, do go back to the beginning of the chapter. And you should feel free to do this at any point when you feel that constructing a sentence is becoming a struggle. There is no rush. You should always only work at a pace that feels suitable to you. And when you do get to the point where you can get through this entire dialogue without making any mistakes, it can still be worth practising it a few times. This will help build your fluency and confidence in using what you've learnt.

If you've done all that then you can look forward to expanding and developing this dialogue even further as you venture into the next chapter.

Building Blocks 3

It's time again to add some new building blocks. Here they are:

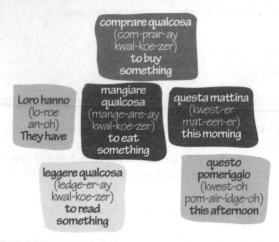

comprare qualcosa
(com-prar-ay
kwal-koe-zer)
**to buy
something**

Loro hanno
(lo-roe
an-oh)
They have

mangiare
qualcosa
(mange-are-ay
kwal-koe-zer)
**to eat
something**

questa mattina
(kwest-er
mat-een-er)
this morning

leggere qualcosa
(ledge-er-ay
kwal-koe-zer)
**to read
something**

questo
pomeriggio
(kwest-oh
pom-air-idge-oh)
this afternoon

You now have your new building blocks. Make as many sentences as you can!

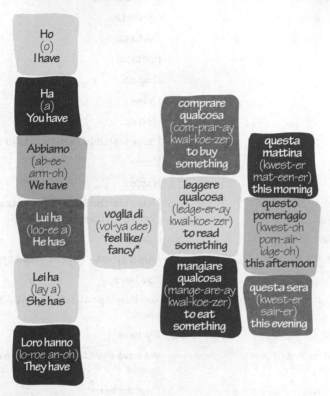

Ho
(o)
I have

Ha
(a)
You have

Abbiamo
(ab-ee-arm-oh)
We have

Lui ha
(loo-ee a)
He has

Lei ha
(lay a)
She has

Loro hanno
(lo-roe an-oh)
They have

voglia di
(vol-ya dee)
feel like/fancy*

comprare qualcosa
(com-prar-ay kwal-koe-zer)
to buy something

leggere qualcosa
(ledge-er-ay kwal-koe-zer)
to read something

mangiare qualcosa
(mange-are-ay kwal-koe-zer)
to eat something

questa mattina
(kwest-er mat-een-er)
this morning

questo pomeriggio
(kwest-oh pom-air-idge-oh)
this afternoon

questa sera
(kwest-er sair-er)
this evening

* literally "want of"

Checklist 3

You know what to do with the checklist now, so you don't need to be reminded about that.

Do bear one thing in mind though. The checklists don't need to be done in one sitting. So, if you get through a page or two and feel that's enough, then simply leave the rest until the next day. Always work at your own pace and don't do so much that you end up feeling overwhelmed. "Steady as she goes" should be your mantra!

il weekend (eel weekend)	the weekend
romantico (roe-man-teek-oh)	romantic
fantastico (fan-tass-teek-oh)	fantastic
politico (pol-ee-teek-oh)	political
illogico (ee-lodge-eek-oh)	illogical
Ho (o)	I have
visitato (visit-art-oh)	visited
Ho visitato (o visit-art-oh)	I have visited / I visited / I did visit
Roma (roam-er)	Rome
Napoli (nap-oh-lee)	Naples
Ho visitato Napoli. (o visit-art-oh nap-oh-lee)	I have visited Naples / I visited Naples / I did visit Naples.
passato (pass-art-oh)	spent
Ho passato (o pass-art-oh)	I have spent / I spent / I did spend
Ha (a)	You have
Ha passato (a pass-art-oh)	You have spent / You spent / You did spend
Abbiamo (ab-ee-arm-oh)	We have
Abbiamo passato (ab-ee-arm-oh pass-art-oh)	We have spent / We spent / We did spend
settembre (se-tem-bray)	September
il Natale (eel nat-arl-ay)	Christmas
a Roma (a roam-er)	in Rome
in Italia (een eet-al-yer)	in Italy
in Svizzera (een zvee-tser-er)	in Switzerland
Abbiamo passato il Natale in Svizzera. (ab-ee-arm-oh pass-art-oh eel nat-arl-ay een zvee-tser-er)	We have spent Christmas in Switzerland / We spent Christmas in Switzerland / We did spend Christmas in Switzerland.
Ha passato settembre in Italia. (a pass-art-oh se-tem-bray een eet-al-yer)	You have spent September in Italy / You spent September in Italy / You did spend September in Italy.
e (ay)	and

Era (air-ah)	It was
Era fantastico. (air-ah fan-tass-teek-oh)	It was fantastic.
Il tempo era fantastico. (eel-tem-poe air-ah fan-tass-teek-oh)	The weather was fantastic.
Ho passato il weekend a Roma – e wow, il tempo era fantastico. (o pass-art-oh eel weekend a roam-er ay wow, eel-tem-poe air-ah fan-tass-teek-oh)	I spent the weekend in Rome – and wow, the weather was fantastic.
preparazione (prep-are-atz-ee-oh-nay)	preparation
preparato (pray-par-ato)	prepared
prenotazione (pray-no-tatz-ee-oh-nay)	reservation
prenotato (pray-no-tart-oh)	reserved / booked
ordinato (or-din-art-oh)	ordered
pagato (pag-art-oh)	paid
fatto (fat-oh)	done
il conto (eel kon-toe)	the bill
la cena (la chain-er)	the dinner
il caffè (eel ka-fe)	the coffee
un tavolo (oon tav-oh-loe)	a table
una camera (oon-a cam-air-a)	a room
un taxi (oon taxi)	a taxi
Ho preparato la cena. (o prep-are-art-oh la chain-er)	I have prepared the dinner / I prepared the dinner / I did prepare the dinner.
Ho ordinato il caffè per la cena. (o or-din-art-oh eel ka-fe pair la chain-er)	I have ordered coffee for dinner / I ordered coffee for dinner / I did order coffee for dinner.
Ho prenotato un tavolo per Lei. (o pray-no-tart-oh oon tav-oh-loe pair lay)	I have booked a table for you / I booked a table for you / I did book a table for you.

Lei ha (lay a)	She has
Lei ha prenotato un tavolo per questa sera. (lay a pray-no-tart-oh oon tav-oh-loe pair kwest-er sair-er)	She has booked / reserved a table for this evening – She booked / reserved a table for this evening – She did book / reserve a table for this evening.
Lui ha (loo-ee a)	He has
Lui ha prenotato una camera per due persone. (loo-ee a pray-no-tart-oh oon-a cam-air-a pair doo-ay pair-soan-ay)	He has booked / reserved a room for two people – He booked / reserved a room for two people – He did book / reserve a room for two people.
Abbiamo prenotato un taxi per Lei. (ab-ee-arm-oh pray-no-tart-oh oon taxi pair lay)	We have booked a taxi for you / We booked a taxi for you / We did book a taxi for you.
Abbiamo pagato il conto. (ab-ee-arm-oh pag-art-oh eel kon-toe)	We paid the bill / We have paid the bill / We did pay the bill.
Che cosa? (ke koe-ser)	What? / What thing?
Che cosa ha preparato? (ke koe-ser a prep-are-art-oh)	What have you prepared? / What did you prepare? (literally "What thing you have prepared?")
Che cosa ha fatto? (ke koe-ser a fat-oh)	What have you done? / What did you do? (literally "What thing you have done?")
Ho prenotato un tavolo, ordinato la cena e poi pagato il conto. Che cosa ha fatto? (o pray-no-tart-oh oon tav-oh-loe, or-din-art-oh la chain-er ey poy pag-art-oh eel kon-toe. ke koe-ser a fat-oh)	I booked a table, ordered dinner and then paid the bill. What did you do?
Ho intenzione di… (o in-ten-tzee-oh-nay dee)	I'm planning to… (literally "I have intention of…")
Ho intenzione di ritornare in Italia a maggio. (o in-ten-tzee-oh-nay dee ri-torn-are-ay een eet-al-yer a madge-oh)	I'm planning to go back to Italy in May.
Ho paura di… (o pow-oo-rer dee)	I'm scared of… (literally "I have fear of…")

Ho paura di ritornare in Italia a settembre. (o pow-oo-rer dee ri-torn-are-ay een eet-al-yer a se-tem-bray)	I'm scared of going back to Italy in September.
Veramente? (ve-ra-men-tay)	Really?
quindi (kwin-dee)	so
ma (mu)	but
Ho voglia di... (o vol-ya dee)	I feel like... / I fancy... (literally "I have want of...")
Sì, ho voglia di ritornare a Roma ma ho paura di volare, quindi ho intenzione di prendere l'Eurostar. (see, o vol-ya dee ri-torn-are-ay a roam-er mu o pow-oo-rer dee vol-are-ay, kwin-dee o in-ten-tzee-oh-nay dee pren-de-rey lay-oo-roe-star)	Yes, I feel like going back to Rome but I'm scared of flying, so I'm planning to take the Eurostar.
Ho voglia di comprare qualcosa questa mattina. (o vol-ya dee com-prar-ay kwal-koe-zer kwest-er mat-een-er)	I feel like / fancy buying something this morning.
Lui ha voglia di leggere qualcosa questo pomeriggio. (loo-ee a vol-ya dee ledge-er-ay kwal-koe-zer kwest-oh pom-air-idge-oh)	He feels like / fancies reading something this afternoon.
Loro hanno (lo-roe an-oh)	They have
Loro hanno voglia di mangiare qualcosa questa sera. (lo-roe an-oh vol-ya dee mange-are-ay kwal-koe-zer kwest-er sair-er)	They feel like eating something this evening.

Now, time to do it the other way around!

the weekend	**il weekend** (eel weekend)
romantic	**romantico** (roe-man-teek-oh)
fantastic	**fantastico** (fan-tass-teek-oh)
political	**politico** (pol-ee-teek-oh)

illogical	**illogico** (ee-lodge-eek-oh)
I have	**Ho** (o)
visited	**visitato** (visit-art-oh)
I have visited / I visited / I did visit	**Ho visitato** (o visit-art-oh)
Rome	**Roma** (roam-er)
Naples	**Napoli** (nap-oh-lee)
I have visited Naples / I visited Naples / I did visit Naples.	**Ho visitato Napoli.** (o visit-art-oh nap-oh-lee)
spent	**passato** (pass-art-oh)
I have spent / I spent / I did spend	**Ho passato** (o pass-art-oh)
You have	**Ha** (a)
You have spent / You spent / You did spend	**Ha passato** (a pass-art-oh)
We have	**Abbiamo** (ab-ee-arm-oh)
We have spent / We spent / We did spend	**Abbiamo passato** (ab-ee-arm-oh pass-art-oh)
September	**settembre** (se-tem-bray)
Christmas	**il Natale** (eel nat-arl-ay)
in Rome	**a Roma** (a roam-er)
in Italy	**in Italia** (een eet-al-yer)
in Switzerland	**in Svizzera** (een zvee-tser-er)
We have spent Christmas in Switzerland / We spent Christmas in Switzerland / We did spend Christmas in Switzerland.	**Abbiamo passato il Natale in Svizzera.** (ab-ee-arm-oh pass-art-oh eel nat-arl-ay een zvee-tser-er)
You have spent September in Italy / You spent September in Italy / You did spend September in Italy.	**Ha passato settembre in Italia.** (a pass-art-oh se-tem-bray een eet-al-yer)
and	**e** (ay)
It was	**Era** (air-ah)
It was fantastic.	**Era fantastico.** (air-ah fan-tass-teek-oh)

The weather was fantastic.	Il **tempo** era fantastico. (eel-tem-poe air-ah fan-tass-teek-oh)
I spent the weekend in Rome – and wow, the weather was fantastic.	Ho **passato** il weekend a Roma – e wow, il tempo era fantastico. (o pass-art-oh eel weekend a roam-er ay wow, eel-tem-poe air-ah fan-tass-teek-oh)
preparation	**preparazione** (prep-are-atz-ee-oh-nay)
prepared	**preparato** (pray-par-ay)
reservation	**prenotazione** (pray-no-tatz-ee-oh-nay)
reserved / booked	**prenotato** (pray-no-tart-oh)
ordered	**ordinato** (or-din-art-oh)
paid	**pagato** (pag-art-oh)
done	**fatto** (fat-oh)
the bill	il **conto** (eel kon-toe)
the dinner	la **cena** (la chain-er)
the coffee	il **caffè** (eel ka-fe)
a table	un **tavolo** (oon tav-oh-loe)
a room	una **camera** (oon-a cam-air-a)
a taxi	un **taxi** (oon taxi)
I have prepared the dinner / I prepared the dinner / I did prepare the dinner.	Ho **preparato** la cena. (o prep-are-art-oh la chain-er)
I have ordered coffee for dinner / I ordered coffee for dinner / I did order coffee for dinner.	Ho **ordinato** il caffè per la cena. (o or-din-art-oh eel ka-fe pair la chain-er)
I have booked a table for you / I booked a table for you / I did book a table for you.	Ho **prenotato** un tavolo per Lei. (o pray-no-tart-oh oon tav-oh-loe pair lay)
She has	Lei ha (lay a)

She has booked / reserved a table for this evening – She booked / reserved a table for this evening – She did book / reserve a table for this evening.	Lei ha prenotato un tavolo per questa sera. (lay a pray-no-tart-oh oon tav-oh-loe pair kwest-er sair-er)
He has	Lui ha (loo-ee a)
He has booked / reserved a room for two people – He booked / reserved a room for two people – He did book / reserve a room for two people.	Lui ha prenotato una camera per due persone. (loo-ee a pray-no-tart-oh oon-a cam-air-a pair doo-ay pair-soan-ay)
We have booked a taxi for you / We booked a taxi for you / We did book a taxi for you.	Abbiamo prenotato un taxi per Lei. (ab-ee-arm-oh pray-no-tart-oh oon taxi pair lay)
We paid the bill / We have paid the bill / We did pay the bill.	Abbiamo pagato il conto. (ab-ee-arm-oh pag-art-oh eel kon-toe)
What? / What thing?	Che cosa? (ke koe-ser)
What have you prepared? / What did you prepare? (literally "What thing you have prepared?")	Che cosa ha preparato? (ke koe-ser a prep-are-art-oh)
What have you done? / What did you do? (literally "What thing you have done?")	Che cosa ha fatto? (ke koe-ser a fat-oh)
I booked a table, ordered dinner and then paid the bill. What did you do?	Ho prenotato un tavolo, ordinato la cena e poi pagato il conto. Che cosa ha fatto? (o pray-no-tart-oh oon tav-oh-loe, or-din-art-oh la chain-er ey poy pag-art-oh eel kon-toe. ke koe-ser a fat-oh)
I'm planning to… (literally "I have intention of…")	Ho intenzione di… (o in-ten-tzee-oh-nay dee)
I'm planning to go back to Italy in May.	Ho intenzione di ritornare in Italia a maggio. (o in-ten-tzee-oh-nay dee ri-torn-are-ay een eet-al-yer a madge-oh)
I'm scared of… (literally "I have fear of…")	Ho paura di… (o pow-oo-rer dee)

I'm scared of going back to Italy in September.	Ho paura di ritornare in Italia a settembre. (o pow-oo-rer dee ri-torn-are-ay een eet-al-yer a se-tem-bray)
Really?	Veramente? (ve-ra-men-tay)
so	quindi (kwin-dee)
but	ma (mu)
I feel like… / I fancy… (literally "I have want of…")	Ho voglia di… (o vol-ya dee)
Yes, I feel like going back to Rome but I'm scared of flying, so I'm planning to take the Eurostar.	Sì, ho voglia di ritornare a Roma ma ho paura di volare, quindi ho intenzione di prendere l'Eurostar. (see, o vol-ya dee ri-torn-are-ay a roam-er mu o pow-oo-rer dee vol-are-ay, kwin-dee o in-ten-tzee-oh-nay dee pren-de-rey lay-oo-roe-star)
I feel like / fancy buying something this morning.	Ho voglia di comprare qualcosa questa mattina. (o vol-ya dee com-prar-ay kwal-koe-zer kwest-er mat-een-er
He feels like / fancies reading something this afternoon.	Lui ha voglia di leggere qualcosa questo pomeriggio. (loo-ee a vol-ya dee ledge-er-ay kwal-koe-zer kwest-oh pom-air-idge-oh)
They have	Loro hanno (lo-roe an-oh)
They feel like eating something this evening.	Loro hanno voglia di mangiare qualcosa questa sera. (lo-roe an-oh vol-ya dee mange-are-ay kwal-koe-zer kwest-er sair-er)

Well, that's it, you're done with Chapter 3! Take a break!

How to learn the Italian days of the week in an easy and meaningful way!

Do you know the days of the week in Italian?

Well, whether you do or don't, most people are very rarely aware of what the days of the week actually mean in Italian. If they did, they might be surprised how much easier to remember, more meaningful and more beautiful they become.

Let's take a look at them!

Monday – lunedì

Monday, in English, actually means "Moon's Day" and the same is true in Italian. The Italians use part of their word for moon, which is "luna" (think "lunar") and then add the Latin word for "day" to the end of it, making "lunedì" – Moonday / Monday.

Tuesday – martedì

If Monday in Italian is dedicated to the moon, Tuesday is dedicated to Mars. To make Tuesday in Italian we take the Italian word for Mars, "Marte", and add the Latin word for "day" to the end of it, making "martedì" – Mars's Day / Tuesday.

Wednesday – mercoledì

Ah, here we are now at Wednesday or "Woden's Day" as it really should read in English. Whereas in English Wednesday celebrates the god Woden, in Italian it celebrates Mercury, making Wednesday Mercury's Day in Italian – "mercoledì".

Thursday – giovedì

In English, the day after Woden's Day is of course "Thor's Day", now written Thursday. In Italian, by contrast, the day belongs to Jove, king of the gods. Jove's Day in Italian is "giovedì".

Friday – venerdì

Friday in English means "Frigga's Day". "Who is Frigga?" you may ask. Well, she was Odin's wife and Thor's mother. She was also, for the earliest English people, the goddess of love. Curiously, Italian also names Friday after a goddess of love, Venus. So, Friday in Italian is Venus's Day – "venerdì".

Saturday – sabato

Saturday in English is "Saturn's Day". The Italian for Saturday, however, simply means "sabbath", as the sabbath was originally observed on Saturday rather than Sunday. So, Saturday in Italian is "sabato".

Sunday – domenica

I'm sure you can guess the meaning of Sunday in English; clearly it is the Sun's Day. In Italian though its name comes from Latin again – this time from "diēs Dominica" – meaning "the day of the Lord". In modern Italian this has simply become "domenica".

So, there you have the days of the week in Italian. Hopefully they hold a little more meaning for you than they did before. If you don't know them already, you'll find them on a quick reference list on the next page. Just take a look at it each time you finish a chapter, covering up the Italian and seeing if you can recall it, and you'll soon pick them up.

(By the way, have you noticed that, unlike in English, days of the week in Italian don't need to be written with a capital letter?)

Monday	Moon Day	lunedì	
Tuesday	Mars Day	martedì	
Wednesday	Mercury Day	mercoledì	
Thursday	Jove Day	giovedì	
Friday	Venus Day	venerdì	
Saturday	Sabbath Day	sabato	
Sunday	Day of the Lord	domenica	

CHAPTER 4

You need help, mate!

You need help, mate!

Person 1:	I'm planning to go back to Italy in May.
Person 2:	Really?
Person 1:	Yes, I feel like going back to Rome but I'm scared of flying, so I'm planning to take the Eurostar.
Person 2:	Really? You're scared of flying?
Person 1:	Yes, I can't stand planes!
Person 2:	You need help, mate!

As you can see, I have extended the dialogue from the previous chapter. You are now going to learn how to complete this conversation by building on what you've learnt already. You will also expand your range of everyday Italian expressions as you go.

So, remind me now, how would you say "I'm planning to..."?

Ho intenzione di...
(o in-ten-tzee-oh-nay dee)

And how would you say "I'm planning to go back to Italy in May"?

Ho intenzione di ritornare in Italia a maggio.
(o in-ten-tzee-oh-nay dee ri-torn-are-ay een eet-al-yer a madge-oh)

How would someone reply to that, saying "really"?

Veramente?
(ve-ra-men-tay)

And again, what was "I feel like..." in Italian?

Ho voglia di...
(o vol-ya dee)

So how would you say "I feel like going back to Italy / I fancy going back to Italy"?

Ho voglia di ritornare in Italia.
(*o vol-ya dee ri-torn-are-ay een eet-al-yer*)

How about "I feel like going back to Rome / I fancy going back to Rome"?

Ho voglia di ritornare a Roma.
(*o vol-ya dee ri-torn-are-ay a roam-er*)

And how would you say "I'm scared of..." in Italian?

Ho paura di...
(*o pow-oo-rer dee*)

What about "I'm scared of flying"?

Ho paura di volare.
(*o pow-oo-rer dee vol-are-ay*)

Finally, just as at the end of the previous chapter, give an answer saying "Yes, I feel like going back to Rome but I'm scared of flying, so I'm planning to take the Eurostar".

Sì, ho voglia di ritornare a Roma ma ho paura di volare, quindi ho intenzione di prendere l'Eurostar.
(see, o vol-ya dee ri-torn-are-ay a roam-er mu o pow-oo-rer dee vol-are-ay, kwin-dee o in-ten-tzee-oh-nay dee pren-de-rey lay-oo-roe-star)

In the first part of the dialogue you learnt "I'm planning to..." (literally "I have intention of..."), which was:

Ho intenzione di...
(o in-ten-tzee-oh-nay dee)

You also learnt "I feel like... / I fancy..." (literally "I have want of..."), which was:

Ho voglia di...
(o vol-ya dee)

And finally you learnt "I'm scared of..." (literally "I have fear of..."), which was:

Ho paura di...
(o pow-oo-rer dee)

These are all useful phrases that are constructed in a similar way. I'm going to introduce you to just two more similarly structured phrases, so that you can complete the dialogue. As you're familiar with how these types of phrases work already, you should find using them pretty easy.

To say "I can't stand..." in Italian, you will literally say "I have the horror of...", which in Italian is:

Ho l'orrore di...
(o lo-roar-ay dee)

So, to say "I can't stand flying!", for instance, you will literally say "I have the horror of to fly!" How do you think you would say that?

Ho l'orrore di volare!
(*o lo-roar-ay dee vol-are-ay*)

And what was "to take the Eurostar" in Italian?

prendere l'Eurostar
(*pren-de-rey lay-oo-roe-star*)

So, how would you say "I can't stand taking the Eurostar!" (literally "I have the horror of to take the Eurostar!"?

Ho l'orrore di prendere l'Eurostar!
(*o lo-roar-ay dee pren-de-rey lay-oo-roe-star*)

Again, what is "we have"?

Abbiamo
(*ab-ee-arm-oh*)

So, how would you say "we can't stand taking the Eurostar!" (literally "we have the horror of to take the Eurostar")?

Abbiamo l'orrore di prendere l'Eurostar!
(*ab-ee-arm-oh lo-roar-ay dee pren-de-rey lay-oo-roe-star*)

How about "we can't stand flying!"?

Abbiamo l'orrore di volare!
(*ab-ee-arm-oh lo-roar-ay dee vol-are-ay*)

What is "he has"?

Lui ha
(*loo-ee a*)

How would you say "he can't stand flying!"?

Lui ha l'orrore di volare!
(loo-ee a lo-roar-ay dee vol-are-ay)

What is "she has"?

Lei ha
(lay a)

So how would you say "she can't stand flying!"?

Lei ha l'orrore di volare!
(el a lo-roar-ay dee vol-are-ay)

What is "they have"?

Loro hanno
(lo-roe an-oh)

And "they can't stand flying!"?

Loro hanno l'orrore di volare!
(lo-roe an-oh lo-roar-ay dee vol-are-ay)

Finally, what is "you have"?

Ha
(a)

So how would you say "you can't stand flying!"?

Ha l'orrore di volare!
(a lo-roar-ay dee vol-are-ay)

You can very easily turn this statement "you can't stand flying!" into a question in Italian. All you need to do is raise your voice at the end of the sentence. By doing this, you will ask "you can't stand flying?" – literally "you have the horror of to fly?". Do that now:

Ha l'orrore di volare?
(a lo-roar-ay dee vol-are-ay)

Now try "you can't stand taking the Eurostar?" (literally "you have the horror of to take the Eurostar?"):

Ha l'orrore di prendere l'Eurostar?
(a lo-roar-ay dee pren-de-rey lay-oo-roe-star)

How to say "you" in Italian

So far, you have been using "ha" to mean "you have" in Italian.

However, "ha" is not the only way to say "you have" in Italian. In fact, it is the formal way to do so. So, if you're meeting another person for the first time, or if you're talking to someone you do not know very well, you will use "ha" when you need to say "you have…".

However, if you make a close friend, or if you have family in Italy, you will not use "ha", instead, you will use the informal, familiar way to say "you have", which is "hai".

Let's start using this below.

"You have" (informal) in Italian is:

Hai
(eye[2])

So how would you say "you can't stand taking the Eurostar" (informal)?

Hai l'orrore di prendere l'Eurostar.
(eye lo-roar-ay dee pren-de-rey lay-oo-roe-star)

And how would you say "you can't stand flying" (informal)?

Hai l'orrore di volare.
(eye lo-roar-ay dee vol-are-ay)

How about "you're scared of flying" (informal) – (literally "you have fear of to fly")?

Hai paura di volare.
(eye pow-oo-rer dee vol-are-ay)

---

2   Just to make this clear, in case you're not 100% sure how to pronounce "hai", it is pronounced just like the English word **"eye"**, as in "he has good **eye**sight".

Turn this into a question now by raising your voice at the end of the sentence.
Ask "you're scared of flying?" (informal):

Hai paura di volare?
(eye pow-oo-rer dee vol-are-ay)

And again, how would you say "I'm scared of flying"?

Ho paura di volare.
(o pow-oo-rer dee vol-are-ay)

And "I can't stand flying!" (literally "I have the horror of to fly")?

Ho l'orrore di volare!
(o lo-roar-ay dee vol-are-ay)

Let's assume someone has just asked you if you're scared of flying and you want to
answer, "yes, I can't stand flying!":

Sì, ho l'orrore di volare!
(see, o lo-roar-ay dee vol-are-ay)

Alright, if you have reached this point then you have had plenty of practice saying
"I'm planning to…", "I feel like…", "I can't stand…" and "I'm frightened of…".

Now, as I've said before, please don't try to memorise these phrases or even
make any effort to remember them. All you need to do is work your way through
this book and follow its instructions. Everything introduced will come up again,
multiple times. Sometimes you will forget things as I introduce new words and
constructions but this is all part of the method that I am using to teach you.

So, let's introduce the final phrase from this group of similarly constructed
expressions and head on towards the end of the chapter.

This time you're going to learn how to say "I need…", which in Italian is literally
"I have need of…":

Ho bisogno di…
(o beez-on-yoe dee)

So, how would you say "I need a taxi" (literally "I have need of a taxi")?

Ho bisogno di un taxi.
(o beez-on-yoe dee oon taxi)

And again, what is "a room" in Italian?

una camera
(*oon-a cam-air-a*)

How would you say "I need a room"?

Ho bisogno di una camera.
(*o beez-on-yoe dee oon-a cam-air-a*)

"To speak" or "to talk" in Italian is:

parlare
(*par-lar-ay*)

So, how would you say "I need to speak" (literally "I have need of to speak")?

Ho bisogno di parlare.
(*o beez-on-yoe dee par-lar-ay*)

"Italian" in Italian is:

italiano
(*eet-al-ee-arn-oh*)

How would you say "I need to speak Italian"?

Ho bisogno di parlare italiano.
(*o beez-on-yoe dee par-lar-ay eet-al-ee-arn-oh*)

Now, what is "you have" (formal)?

Ha
(*a*)

And what is "you have" (informal)?

Hai
(*eye*)

So how would you say "you need to speak Italian" (informal) – (literally "you have need of to speak Italian")?

Hai bisogno di parlare italiano.
(*eye beez-on-yoe dee par-lar-ay eet-al-ee-arn-oh*)

How about "you need a room" (informal) – (literally "you have need of a room")?

Hai bisogno di una camera.
(*eye beez-on-yoe dee oon-a cam-air-a*)

What about "you need a taxi" (informal)?

Hai bisogno di un taxi.
(*eye beez-on-yoe dee oon taxi*)

"Help" in Italian is related to the English word "aid", which in Italian is:

aiuto
(*eye-oot-oh*)

So, how would you say "you need help!" (informal)?

Hai bisogno di aiuto!
(*eye bisogno di eye-oot-oh*)

The word for "mate", "pal", "buddy" and so on in Italian is:

amico
(*am-ee-koe*)

Okay, how would you say "you need help, mate!"?

Hai bisogno di aiuto, amico!
(*eye bisogno di eye-oot-oh, am-ee-koe*)

Alright, let's review some of these phrases again.
First of all, how would you say "I'm planning to..."?

Ho intenzione di...
(*o in-ten-tzee-oh-nay dee*)

And how would you say "I feel like... / I fancy..."?

Ho voglia di...
(o vol-ya dee)

How about "I'm scared of..."?

Ho paura di...
(o pow-oo-rer dee)

And "I can't stand..."?

Ho l'orrore di...
(o lo-roar-ay dee)

And finally "I need..."?

Ho bisogno di...
(o beez-on-yoe dee)

How would you say "I need to speak Italian"?

Ho bisogno di parlare italiano.
(o beez-on-yoe dee par-lar-ay eet-al-ee-arn-oh)

What about "I feel like speaking Italian"?

Ho voglia di parlare italiano.
(o vol-ya dee par-lar-ay eet-al-ee-arn-oh)

And "I'm scared of speaking Italian"?

Ho paura di parlare italiano.
(o pow-oo-rer dee par-lar-ay eet-al-ee-arn-oh)

And "I'm planning to speak Italian"?

Ho intenzione di parlare italiano.
(o in-ten-tzee-oh-nay dee par-lar-ay eet-al-ee-arn-oh)

And how would you say "I'm planning to go back to Italy in May"?

Ho intenzione di ritornare in Italia a maggio.
(o in-ten-tzee-oh-nay dee ri-torn-are-ay een eet-al-yer a madge-oh)

How about "I'm scared of going back to Italy in May"?

Ho paura di ritornare in Italia a maggio.
(o pow-oo-rer dee ri-torn-are-ay een eet-al-yer a madge-oh)

What about "I feel like going back to Italy in May"?

Ho voglia di ritornare in Italia a maggio.
(o vol-ya dee ri-torn-are-ay een eet-al-yer a madge-oh)

And "I need to go back to Italy in May"?

Ho bisogno di ritornare in Italia a maggio.
(o beez-on-yoe dee ri-torn-are-ay een eet-al-yer
a madge-oh)

You are probably starting to get a feel now for just
how useful – and interchangable – these phrases
are, depending on what exactly it is you want to say.

Now again, how would you say "I can't stand
flying!"?

Ho l'orrore di volare!
(o lo-roar-ay dee vol-are-ay)

And how would you say "I can't stand taking the
Eurostar!"?

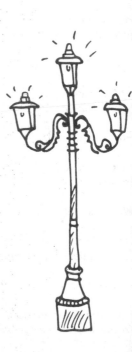

Ho l'orrore di prendere l'Eurostar!
(o lo-roar-ay dee pren-de-rey lay-oo-roe-star)

How would someone you said that to ask you
"really?"?

Veramente?
(ve-ra-men-tay)

And how would you say "I'm planning to take the Eurostar"?

Ho intenzione di prendere l'Eurostar.
(o in-ten-tzee-oh-nay dee pren-de-rey lay-oo-roe-star)

How about "I feel like going back to Rome"?

Ho voglia di ritornare a Roma.
(*o vol-ya dee ri-torn-are-ay a roam-er*)

And what about "I'm scared of flying"?

Ho paura di volare.
(*o pow-oo-rer dee vol-are-ay*)

What is the word for "but" in Italian?

ma
(mu)

And what is the word for "so"?

quindi
(kwin-dee)

So how would you say "I feel like going back to Rome but I'm scared of flying, so I'm planning to take the Eurostar"?

Ho voglia di ritornare a Roma ma ho paura di volare, quindi ho intenzione di prendere l'Eurostar.
(*o vol-ya dee ri-torn-are-ay a roam-er mu o pow-oo-rer dee vol-are-ay, kwin-dee o in-ten-tzee-oh-nay dee pren-de-rey lay-oo-roe-star*)

What is "you have" (informal)?

Hai
(eye)

So how would you say informally "you feel like going back to Rome" (literally "you have want of to return to Rome")?

Hai voglia di ritornare a Roma.
(*eye vol-ya dee ri-torn-are-ay a roam-er*)

How about "you are scared of flying" (informal)?

Hai paura di volare.
(*eye pow-oo-rer dee vol-are-ay*)

Turn this into a question now by raising your voice at the end and ask "you are scared of flying?" (informal):

Hai paura di volare?
(*eye pow-oo-rer dee vol-are-ay*)

How would someone answer this question, saying "Yes, I can't stand flying!"?

Sì, ho l'orrore di volare!
(*see, o lo-roar-ay dee vol-are-ay*)

And again, how would you say "I need…"
(literally "I have need of…")?

Ho bisogno di…
(*o beez-on-yoe dee*)

And so how would you say "I need help"
(literally "I have need of aid")?

Ho bisogno di aiuto.
(*o bisogno di eye-oot-oh*)

And how would you say informally "You need help" (literally "you have need of aid")?

Hai bisogno di aiuto.
(*eye bisogno di eye-oot-oh*)

And what is "friend" or "mate"?

amico
(*am-ee-koe*)

Put this together now and say "You need help, mate!" (informal):

Hai bisogno di aiuto, amico!
(*eye bisogno di eye-oot-oh, am-ee-koe*)

Okay, you're ready now to make an attempt at doing the entire dialogue by yourself. Take each sentence slowly and, if you get it wrong, just take another stab at it. It isn't a race and you should just take your time to work it out.

Have a go now:

Person 1: I'm planning to go back to Italy in May.
Ho intenzione di ritornare in Italia a maggio.
(o in-ten-tzee-oh-nay dee ri-torn-are-ay een eet-al-yer a madge-oh)

Person 2: Really?
Veramente?
(ve-ra-men-tay)

Person 1: Yes, I feel like going back to Rome but I'm scared of flying, so I'm planning to take the Eurostar.
Sì, ho voglia di ritornare a Roma ma ho paura di volare, quindi ho intenzione di prendere l'Eurostar.
(see, o vol-ya dee ri-torn-are-ay a roam-er mu o pow-oo-rer dee vol-are-ay, kwin-dee o in-ten-tzee-oh-nay dee pren-de-rey lay-oo-roe-star)

Person 2: Really? You're scared of flying?
Veramente? Hai paura di volare?
(ve-ra-men-tay eye pow-oo-rer dee vol-are-ay)

Person 1: Yes, I can't stand planes!
Sì, ho l'orrore di volare!
(see, o lo-roar-ay dee vol-are-ay)

Person 2: You need help, mate!
Hai bisogno di aiuto, amico!
(eye bisogno di eye-oot-oh, am-ee-koe)

How did that go? It's fairly complex stuff but as you're probably beginning to notice it is also just a matter of patterns. Learn the patterns and you'll find you can very quickly begin to communicate in the language – and with a minimum of effort!

Building Blocks 4

Okay, building block time. Here they are:

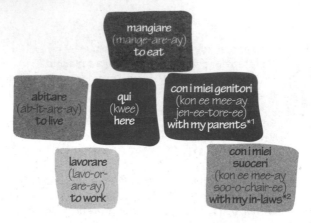

mangiare
(mange-are-ay)
to eat

abitare
(ab-it-are-ay)
to live

qui
(kwee)
here

con i miei genitori
(kon ee mee-ay
jen-ee-tore-ee)
with my parents*1

lavorare
(lavo-or-
are-ay)
to work

**con i miei
suoceri**
(kon ee mee-ay
soo-o-chair-ee)
with my in-laws*2

*1 literally "with the my parents"

*2 literally "with the my in-laws"

As before, use the building blocks below to make as many sentences as you can. Make sure to use every word at least once or, preferably, several times.

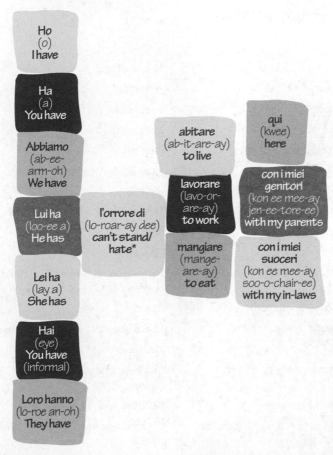

Ho
(o)
I have

Ha
(a)
You have

Abbiamo
(ab-ee-arm-oh)
We have

Lui ha
(loo-ee a)
He has

Lei ha
(lay a)
She has

Hai
(eye)
You have
(informal)

Loro hanno
(lo-roe an-oh)
They have

l'orrore di
(lo-roar-ay dee)
can't stand/
hate*

abitare
(ab-it-are-ay)
to live

lavorare
(lavo-or-are-ay)
to work

mangiare
(mange-are-ay)
to eat

qui
(kwee)
here

con i miei
genitori
(kon ee mee-ay
jen-ee-tore-ee)
with my parents

con i miei
suoceri
(kon ee mee-ay
soo-o-chair-ee)
with my in-laws

* literally "have the horror of"

well, off you go then!

il weekend (eel weekend)	the weekend
romantico (roe-man-teek-oh)	romantic
fantastico (fan-tass-teek-oh)	fantastic
politico (pol-ee-teek-oh)	political
illogico (ee-lodge-eek-oh)	illogical
Ho (o)	I have
visitato (visit-art-oh)	visited
Ho visitato (o visit-art-oh)	I have visited / I visited / I did visit
Roma (roam-er)	Rome
Napoli (nap-oh-lee)	Naples
Ho visitato Napoli. (o visit-art-oh nap-oh-lee)	I have visited Naples / I visited Naples / I did visit Naples.
passato (pass-art-oh)	spent
Ho passato (o pass-art-oh)	I have spent / I spent / I did spend
Ha (a)	You have
Ha passato (a pass-art-oh)	You have spent / You spent / You did spend
Abbiamo (ab-ee-arm-oh)	We have
Abbiamo passato (ab-ee-arm-oh pass-art-oh)	We have spent / We spent / We did spend
settembre (se-tem-bray)	September
il Natale (eel nat-arl-ay)	Christmas
a Roma (a roam-er)	in Rome
in Italia (een eet-al-yer)	in Italy
in Svizzera (een zvee-tser-er)	in Switzerland

Abbiamo passato il Natale in Svizzera. (ab-ee-arm-oh pass-art-oh eel nat-arl-ay een zvee-tser-er)	We have spent Christmas in Switzerland / We spent Christmas in Switzerland / We did spend Christmas in Switzerland.
Ha passato settembre in Italia. (a pass-art-oh se-tem-bray een eet-al-yer)	You have spent September in Italy / You spent September in Italy / You did spend September in Italy.
e (ay)	and
Era (air-ah)	It was
Era fantastico. (air-ah fan-tass-teek-oh)	It was fantastic.
Il tempo era fantastico. (eel-tem-poe air-ah fan-tass-teek-oh)	The weather was fantastic.
Ho passato il weekend a Roma – e wow, il tempo era fantastico. (o pass-art-oh eel weekend a roam-er ay wow, eel-tem-poe air-ah fan-tass-teek-oh)	I spent the weekend in Rome – and wow, the weather was fantastic.
preparazione (prep-are-atz-ee-oh-nay)	preparation
preparato (pray-par-ato)	prepared
prenotazione (pray-no-tatz-ee-oh-nay)	reservation
prenotato (pray-no-tart-oh)	reserved / booked
ordinato (or-din-art-oh)	ordered
pagato (pag-art-oh)	paid
fatto (fat-oh)	done
il conto (eel kon-toe)	the bill
la cena (la chain-er)	the dinner
il caffè (eel ka-fe)	the coffee
un tavolo (oon tav-oh-loe)	a table
una camera (oon-a cam-air-a)	a room
un taxi (oon taxi)	a taxi

Ho preparato la cena. (o prep-are-art-oh la chain-er)	I have prepared the dinner / I prepared the dinner / I did prepare the dinner.
Ho ordinato il caffè per la cena. (o or-din-art-oh eel ka-fe pair la chain-er)	I have ordered coffee for dinner / I ordered coffee for dinner / I did order coffee for dinner.
Ho prenotato un tavolo per Lei. (o pray-no-tart-oh oon tav-oh-loe pair lay)	I have booked a table for you / I booked a table for you / I did book a table for you.
Lei ha (lay a)	She has
Lei ha prenotato un tavolo per questa sera. (lay a pray-no-tart-oh oon tav-oh-loe pair kwest-er sair-er)	She has booked / reserved a table for this evening – She booked / reserved a table for this evening – She did book / reserve a table for this evening.
Lui ha (loo-ee a)	He has
Lui ha prenotato una camera per due persone. (loo-ee a pray-no-tart-oh oon-a cam-air-a pair doo-ay pair-soan-ay)	He has booked / reserved a room for two people – He booked / reserved a room for two people – He did book / reserve a room for two people.
Abbiamo prenotato un taxi per Lei. (ab-ee-arm-oh pray-no-tart-oh oon taxi pair lay)	We have booked a taxi for you / We booked a taxi for you / We did book a taxi for you.
Abbiamo pagato il conto. (ab-ee-arm-oh pag-art-oh eel kon-toe)	We paid the bill / We have paid the bill / We did pay the bill.
Che cosa? (ke koe-ser)	What? / What thing?
Che cosa ha preparato? (ke koe-ser a prep-are-art-oh)	What have you prepared? / What did you prepare? (literally "What thing you have prepared?")
Che cosa ha fatto? (ke koe-ser a fat-oh)	What have you done? / What did you do? (literally "What thing you have done?")
Ho prenotato un tavolo, ordinato la cena e poi pagato il conto. Che cosa ha fatto? (o pray-no-tart-oh oon tav-oh-loe, or-din-art-oh la chain-er ey poy pag-art-oh eel kon-toe. ke koe-ser a fat-oh)	I booked a table, ordered dinner and then paid the bill. What did you do?

Ho intenzione di… (o in-ten-tzee-oh-nay dee)	I'm planning to… (literally "I have intention of…")
Ho intenzione di ritornare in Italia a maggio. (o in-ten-tzee-oh-nay dee ri-torn-are-ay een eet-al-yer a madge-oh)	I'm planning to go back to Italy in May.
Ho paura di… (o pow-oo-rer dee)	I'm scared of… (literally "I have fear of…")
Ho paura di ritornare in Italia a settembre. (o pow-oo-rer dee ri-torn-are-ay een eet-al-yer a se-tem-bray)	I'm scared of going back to Italy in September.
Veramente? (ve-ra-men-tay)	Really?
quindi (kwin-dee)	so
ma (ma)	but
Ho voglia di… (o vol-ya dee)	I feel like… / I fancy… (literally "I have want of…")
Sì, ho voglia di ritornare a Roma ma ho paura di volare, quindi ho intenzione di prendere l'Eurostar. (see, o vol-ya dee ri-torn-are-ay a roam-er ma o pow-oo-rer dee vol-are-ay, kwin-dee o in-ten-tzee-oh-nay dee pren-de-rey lay-oo-roe-star)	Yes, I feel like going back to Rome but I'm scared of flying, so I'm planning to take the Eurostar.
Ho voglia di comprare qualcosa questa mattina. (o vol-ya dee com-prar-ay kwal-koe-zer kwest-er mat-een-er	I feel like / fancy buying something this morning.
Lui ha voglia di leggere qualcosa questo pomeriggio. (loo-ee a vol-ya dee ledge-er-ay kwal-koe-zer kwest-oh pom-air-idge-oh)	He feels like / fancies reading something this afternoon.
Loro hanno (lo-roe an-oh)	They have
Loro hanno voglia di mangiare qualcosa questa sera. (lo-roe an-oh vol-ya dee mange-are-ay kwal-koe-zer kwest-er sair-er)	They feel like / fancy eating something this evening.

Ho bisogno di... (o beez-on-yoe dee)	I need... (literally "I have need of...")
Ho bisogno di parlare italiano. (o beez-on-yoe dee par-lar-ay eet-al-ee-arn-oh)	I need to speak Italian.
Ho bisogno di un taxi. (o beez-on-yoe dee oon taxi)	I need a taxi.
Ho bisogno di una camera. (o beez-on-yoe dee oon-a cam-air-a)	I need a room.
Ho bisogno di aiuto. (o bisogno di eye-oot-oh)	I need help.
Hai bisogno di aiuto, amico! (eye bisogno di eye-oot-oh am-ee-koe)	You need help, mate!
Ho l'orrore di... (o lo-roar-ay dee)	I can't stand... / I hate... (literally "I have the horror of...")
Ho l'orrore di volare! (o lo-roar-ay dee vol-are-ay)	I can't stand flying! / I hate flying!
Ho l'orrore di abitare con i miei suoceri. (o lo-roar-ay dee ab-it-are-ay kon ee mee-ay soo-o-chair-ee)	I can't stand living with my in-laws / I hate living with my in-laws.
Abbiamo l'orrore di mangiare con i miei genitori. (ab-ee-arm-oh lo-roar-ay dee mange-are-ay kon ee mee-ay jen-ee-tore-ee)	We can't stand eating with my parents / We hate eating with my parents.
Lei ha l'orrore di lavorare qui. (lay a lo-roar-ay dee lavo-or-are-ay kwee)	She can't stand working here / She hates working here.

Now, time to do it the other way around!

the weekend	il weekend (eel weekend)
romantic	romantico (roe-man-teek-oh)
fantastic	fantastico (fan-tass-teek-oh)
political	politico (pol-ee-teek-oh)
illogical	illogico (ee-lodge-eek-oh)
I have	Ho (o)

visited	**visitato** (visit-art-oh)
I have visited / I visited / I did visit	**Ho visitato** (o visit-art-oh)
Rome	**Roma** (roam-er)
Naples	**Napoli** (nap-oh-lee)
I have visited Naples / I visited Naples / I did visit Naples.	**Ho visitato Napoli.** (o visit-art-oh nap-oh-lee)
spent	**passato** (pass-art-oh)
I have spent / I spent / I did spend	**Ho passato** (o pass-art-oh)
You have	**Ha** (a)
You have spent / You spent / You did spend	**Ha passato** (a pass-art-oh)
We have	**Abbiamo** (ab-ee-arm-oh)
We have spent / We spent / We did spend	**Abbiamo passato** (ab-ee-arm-oh pass-art-oh)
September	**settembre** (se-tem-bray)
Christmas	**il Natale** (eel nat-arl-ay)
in Rome	**a Roma** (a roam-er)
in Italy	**in Italia** (een eet-al-yer)
in Switzerland	**in Svizzera** (een zvee-tser-er)
We have spent Christmas in Switzerland / We spent Christmas in Switzerland / We did spend Christmas in Switzerland.	**Abbiamo passato il Natale in Svizzera.** (ab-ee-arm-oh pass-art-oh eel nat-arl-ay een zvee-tser-er)
You have spent September in Italy / You spent September in Italy / You did spend September in Italy.	**Ha passato settembre in Italia.** (a pass-art-oh se-tem-bray een eet-al-yer)
and	**e** (ay)
It was	**Era** (air-ah)
It was fantastic.	**Era fantastico.** (air-ah fan-tass-teek-oh)
The weather was fantastic.	**Il tempo era fantastico.** (eel-tem-poe air-ah fan-tass-teek-oh)

I spent the weekend in Rome – and wow, the weather was fantastic.	Ho passato il weekend a Roma – e wow, il tempo era fantastico. (o pass-art-oh eel weekend a roam-er ay wow, eel-tem-poe air-ah fan-tass-teek-oh)
preparation	preparazione (prep-are-atz-ee-oh-nay)
prepared	preparato (pray-par-ay)
reservation	prenotazione (pray-no-tatz-ee-oh-nay)
reserved / booked	prenotato (pray-no-tart-oh)
ordered	ordinato (or-din-art-oh)
paid	pagato (pag-art-oh)
done	fatto (fat-oh)
the bill	il conto (eel kon-toe)
the dinner	la cena (la chain-er)
the coffee	il caffè (eel ka-fe)
a table	un tavolo (oon tav-oh-loe)
a room	una camera (oon-a cam-air-a)
a taxi	un taxi (oon taxi)
I have prepared the dinner / I prepared the dinner / I did prepare the dinner.	Ho preparato la cena. (o prep-are-art-oh la chain-er)
I have ordered coffee for dinner / I ordered coffee for dinner / I did order coffee for dinner.	Ho ordinato il caffè per la cena. (o or-din-art-oh eel ka fe pair la chain-er)
I have booked a table for you / I booked a table for you / I did book a table for you.	Ho prenotato un tavolo per Lei. (o pray-no-tart-oh oon tav-oh-loe pair lay)
She has	Lei ha (lay a)
She has booked / reserved a table for this evening – She booked / reserved a table for this evening – She did book / reserve a table for this evening.	Lei ha prenotato un tavolo per questa sera. (lay a pray-no-tart-oh oon tav-oh-loe pair kwest-er sair-er)
He has	Lui ha (loo-ee a)

He has booked / reserved a room for two people – He booked / reserved a room for two people – He did book / reserve a room for two people.	**Lui ha prenotato una camera per due persone.** (loo-ee a pray-no-tart-oh oon-a cam-air-a pair doo-ay pair-soan-ay)
We have booked a taxi for you / We booked a taxi for you / We did book a taxi for you.	**Abbiamo prenotato un taxi per Lei.** (ab-ee-arm-oh pray-no-tart-oh oon taxi pair lay)
We paid the bill / We have paid the bill / We did pay the bill.	**Abbiamo pagato il conto.** (ab-ee-arm-oh pag-art-oh eel kon-toe)
What? / What thing?	**Che cosa?** (ke koe-ser)
What have you prepared? / What did you prepare? (literally "What thing you have prepared?")	**Che cosa ha preparato?** (ke koe-ser a prep-are-art-oh)
What have you done? / What did you do? (literally "What thing you have done?")	**Che cosa ha fatto?** (ke koe-ser a fat-oh)
I booked a table, ordered dinner and then paid the bill. What did you do?	**Ho prenotato un tavolo, ordinato la cena e poi pagato il conto. Che cosa ha fatto?** (o pray-no-tart-oh oon tav-oh-loe, or-din-art-oh la chain-er ey poy pag-art-oh eel kon-toe. ke koe-ser a fat-oh)
I'm planning to...	**Ho intenzione di...** (o in-ten-tzee-oh-nay dee)
I'm planning to go back to Italy in May.	**Ho intenzione di ritornare in Italia a maggio.** (o in-ten-tzee-oh-nay dee ri-torn-are-ay een eet-al-yer a madge-oh)
I'm scared of...	**Ho paura di...** (o pow-oo-rer dee)
I'm scared of going back to Italy in September.	**Ho paura di ritornare in Italia a settembre.** (o pow-oo-rer dee ri-torn-are-ay een eet-al-yer a se-tem-bray)
Really?	**Veramente?** (ve-ra-men-tay)
so	**quindi** (kwin-dee)
but	**ma** (mu)
I feel like... / I fancy... (literally "I have want of")	**Ho voglia di...** (o vol-ya dee)

Yes, I feel like / fancy going back to Rome but I'm scared of flying, so I'm planning to take the Eurostar.	**Sì, ho voglia di ritornare a Roma ma ho paura di volare, quindi ho intenzione di prendere l'Eurostar.** (see, o vol-ya dee ri-torn-are-ay a roam-er mu o pow-oo-rer dee vol-are-ay, kwin-dee o in-ten-tzee-oh-nay dee pren-de-rey lay-oo-roe-star)
I feel like / fancy buying something this morning.	**Ho voglia di comprare qualcosa questa mattina.** (o vol-ya dee com-prar-ay kwal-koe-zer kwest-er mat-een-er
He feels like / fancies reading something this afternoon.	**Lui ha voglia di leggere qualcosa questo pomeriggio.** (loo-ee a vol-ya dee ledge-er-ay kwal-koe-zer kwest-oh pom-air-idge-oh)
They have	**Loro hanno** (lo-roe an-oh)
They feel like / fancy eating something this evening.	**Loro hanno voglia di mangiare qualcosa questa sera.** (lo-roe an-oh vol-ya dee mange-arc·ay kwal-koe-zer kwest-er sair-er)
I need… (literally "I have need of…")	**Ho bisogno di…** (o beez-on-yoe dee)
I need to speak Italian.	**Ho bisogno di parlare italiano.** (o beez-on-yoe dee par-lar-ay eet-al-ee-arn-oh)
I need a taxi.	**Ho bisogno di un taxi.** (o beez-on-yoe dee oon taxi)
I need a room.	**Ho bisogno di una camera.** (o beez-on-yoe dee oon-a cam-air-a)
I need help.	**Ho bisogno di aiuto.** (o bisogno di eye-oot-oh)
You need help, mate!	**Hai bisogno di aiuto, amico!** (eye bisogno di eye-oot-oh am-ee-koe)
I can't stand… / I hate… (literally "I have the horror of…")	**Ho l'orrore di…** (o lo-roar-ay dee)
I can't stand flying! / I hate flying!	**Ho l'orrore di volare!** (o lo-roar-ay dee vol-are-ay)

I can't stand living with my in-laws / I hate living with my in-laws.	Ho l'orrore di abitare con i miei suoceri. (o lo-roar-ay dee ab-it-are-ay kon ee mee-ay soo-o-chair-ee)
We can't stand eating with my parents / We hate eating with my parents.	Abbiamo l'orrore di mangiare con i miei genitori. (ab-ee-arm-oh lo-roar-ay dee mange-are-ay kon ee mee-ay jen-ee-tore-ee)
She can't stand working here / She hates working here.	Lei ha l'orrore di lavorare qui. (lay a lo-roar-ay dee lavo-or-are-ay kwee)

Well, that's it, you're done with Chapter 4! Remember, don't try to hold onto or remember anything you've learnt here. Everything you learnt in earlier chapters will be brought back up and reinforced in later chapters. You don't need to do anything or make any effort to memorise anything.

Between Chapters Tip!

Use your "hidden moments"

A famous American linguist, Barry Farber, learnt a large part of the languages he spoke during the "hidden moments" he found in everyday life. Such hidden moments might include the time he spent waiting for a train to arrive, or for the kids to come out of school, or for the traffic to get moving in the morning. These "hidden moments" would otherwise have been useless and unimportant in his daily life but, for someone learning a language, they were some of the most useful minutes of the day.

Breaking up your study time into lots of little bits like this can also help to stop it from feeling like a great effort, or from becoming impractical when your life gets especially hectic.

So, keep this book handy whenever you go out and then make use of such "hidden moments" whenever they come along.

CHAPTER 5

I was just about to book
a taxi when you called me.
Really!

I was just about to book a taxi when you called me. Really!

Well, here we are again. Another chapter, beginning with another simple sentence "I was just about to book a taxi when you called me. Really!" This sentence has some very useful stuff in it and seems basic in English. But, as before, even if you know some Italian already, you may still struggle with constructing it in Italian.

Okay, let's go!

What is "you have" (formal) in Italian?

Ha
(a)

"Called" in Italian is:

chiamato
(kee-am-art-oh)

So, how would you say "you have called"?

Ha chiamato
(a kee-am-art-oh)

And how would you say "you did call"?

Ha chiamato
(a kee-am-art-oh)

And "you called"?

Ha chiamato
(a kee-am-art-oh)

Once again you have three English past tenses for the price of one in Italian. Now, what is "you have" (informal)?

Hai
(*eye*)

How would you say "you have called", "you did call", "you called" (informal)?

Hai *chiamato*
(*eye kee-am-art-oh*)

To recap, just on its own, what is "you have" (informal)?

Hai
(*eye*)

To say "you have me" (informal) in Italian, you will say:

Mi hai
(*mee eye*)

So, literally, this means "me you have". Now, you might be wondering "When am I actually going to need to say 'me you have' in Italian?"

Well, if you want to say, for instance, "you called me" / "you did call me" / "you have called me" in Italian, then you will need to literally say "me you have called".

I'll show you how this works bit by bit just to make it clear.

Again, how would you say "you have" (informal)?

Hai
(*eye*)

And how would you say "you have me" (informal) – (literally "me you have")?

Mi hai
(*mee eye*)

Let's add the word for "called" onto the end of this and by doing so we will say "you called me", "you did call me", "you have called me". So, do that now – say, literally, "me you have called":

Mi hai chiamato.
(*mee eye kee-am-art-oh*)

Let's try this now with "you have" (formal). First though, what is "you have" (formal)?

Ha
(*a*)

And "you have me" (formal) would be:

Mi ha
(*mee a*)

Again, literally, this is "me you have".

So, how do you think you would say "you have called me", "you did call me", "you called me" (formal)?

Mi ha chiamato.
(mee a kee-am-art-oh)

And again, how would you say "you have called me", "you did call me", "you called me" (informal)?

Mi hai chiamato.
(mee eye kee-am-art-oh)

"I was" in Italian is:

Ero
(air-oh)

How would you say "I was romantic"?

Ero romantico.
(air-oh roe-man-teek-oh)

"I was fantastic"?

Ero fantastico.
(air-oh fan-tass-teek-oh)

"I was illogical"?

Ero illogico.
(air-oh ee-lodge-eek-oh)

·Time to steal some words!
Word Robbery Number 3

The third group of words we are going to steal are words that end in **"ary"** in English. These end in **"ario"** in Italian.

In this way, "ordin**ary**" becomes "ordin**ario**", "solit**ary**" becomes "solit**ario**", "contr**ary**" becomes "contr**ario**" and so on.

There are actually more than 400 of these in English and we can begin using these in Italian right away.

Adding them to the words we've already stolen so far, we have now reached a total of 2400 words stolen – and we're only on Chapter 5!

Words stolen so far 2400

So, how would you say "ordinary" in Italian?

ordinario
(or-deen-are-ee-oh)

And "I was ordinary"?

Ero ordinario.
(air-oh or-deen-are-ee-oh)

How about "solitary"?

solitario
(sol-eet-are-ee-oh)

...nd "I was solitary"?

Ero solitario.
(air-oh sol-eet-are-ee-oh)

Good, so we know how to steal these "ary" words from English and use them in Italian.

We also know how to say "I was" in Italian. We can say things like "I was romantic", "I was illogical", "I was ordinary", "I was solitary" and so on.

So, we know "I was". Good. Clear. Understood.

However, there are two useful phrases I want to teach you which use the words "was" in English but which don't use "I was" in Italian.

Instead, they use the words "I stayed". I'll show you what I mean:

To say "I was about to..." or "I was just about to..." in Italian, you won't use "ero" (was) and you also won't use "about to" either. Instead, in Italian, you will literally say "I stayed for...", which is:

Stavo per...
(starve-oh pair)

What is "to reserve" or "to book" in Italian?

Prenotare
(pray-note-are-ay)

And what would "to book a table" be?

Prenotare un tavolo
(pray-note-are-ay oon tav-oh-loe)

And again, what was "I was about to..." / "I was just about to..." (literally "I stayed for...")?

Stavo per...
(starve-oh pair)

So, how would you say "I was about to book a table" (literally "I stayed for to book a table")?

Stavo per prenotare un tavolo.
(starve-oh pair pray-note-are-ay oon tav-oh-loe)

How about "I was about to book a taxi"?

Stavo per prenotare un taxi.
(starve-oh pair pray-note-are-ay oon taxi)

"To prepare" in Italian is:

preparare
(pray-par-are-ay)

So, what would "to prepare the dinner" be?

preparare la cena
(pray-par-are-ay la chain-er)

And how would you say "I was about to prepare the dinner"?

Stavo per preparare la cena.
(starve-oh pair pray-par-are-ay la chain-er)

"To pay" is:

pagare
(pag-are-ay)

How would you say "to pay the bill"?

pagare il conto
(pag-are-ay eel kon-toe)

Now try to say "I was about to pay the bill" (literally "I stayed for to pay the bill"):

Stavo per pagare il conto.
(starve-oh pair pag-are-ay eel kon-toe)

How would you say "I was about to book a taxi"?

Stavo per prenotare un taxi.
(starve-oh pair pray-note-are-ay oon taxi)

And again, what is "you have" (informal)?

Hai
(eye)

And "you have me" (informal)?

Mi hai
(mee eye)

And so how would you say "you have called me", "you did call me", "you called me" (informal) – (literally "me you have called")?

Mi hai chiamato.
(mee eye kee-am-art-oh)

The word for "when" in Italian is:

quando
(kwan-doe)

So, how would you say "...when you called me" (informal)?

...quando mi hai chiamato
(kwan-doe mee eye kee-am-art-oh)

And again, how would you say "I was about to book a taxi"?

Stavo per prenotare un taxi.
(starve-oh pair pray-note-are-ay oon taxi)

Let's put these two parts together now and say "I was about to book a taxi when you called me."

Stavo per prenotare un taxi quando mi hai chiamato.
(starve-oh pair pray-note-are-ay oon taxi kwan-doe mee eye kee-am-art-oh)

If you think the person you're talking to doesn't believe you, you could add something like "really!" onto the end.

What was the Italian word for "really"?

veramente
(ve-ra-men-tay)

So, how would you say "I was about to book a taxi when you called me. Really!"

Stavo per prenotare un taxi quando mi hai chiamato. Veramente!
(starve-oh pair pray-note-are-ay oon taxi kwan-doe mee eye kee-am-art-oh. ve-ra-men-tay)

Well done, another excellent sentence complete!

Building Blocks 5

Here they are:

ordinare un taxi
(or-din-are-ay
oon taxi)
to order a taxi

partire
(part-
ear-ay)
to leave

quando il telefono
ha squillato
(kwan-doe eel
tel-off-on-oh a
skwee-lar-toe)
when the phone rang

quando hai bussato
alla porta
(kwan-doe eye boss-
art-oh al-la port-er)
when you knocked
on the door*1

telefonarti
(tel-ef-own-
are-tee)
telephone you/
to telephone you

quando ha
cominciato a plovere
(kwan-doe a kom-in-
chart-oh a pee-oh-vair-ay)
when it started to rain*2

*1 literally "when you have knocked"

*2 literally "when it has started to rain"

You know what to do!

quando il telefono ha squillato
(kwan-doe eel tel-off-on-oh a skwee-lar-toe)
when the phone rang

partire
(part-ear-ay)
to leave

quando hai bussato alla porta
(kwan-doe eye boss-art-oh al-la port-er)
when you knocked on the door*2

Stavo per
(starve-oh pair)
I was about to*1

ordinare un taxi
(or-din-are-ay oon taxi)
to order a taxi

telefonarti
(tel-ef-own-are-tee)
telephone you/ to telephone you

quando ha cominciato a piovere
(kwan-doe a kom-in-chart-oh a pee-oh-vair-ay)
when it started to rain*3

*1 literally "I stayed for"

*2 literally "when you have knocked at the door"

*3 literally "when it has started to rain"

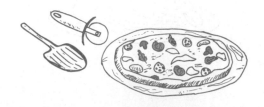

124

Checklist 5

Another chapter finished, another checklist to go through. It's grown very long. Take your time with it. Remember, you don't need to do it all in one go.

il weekend (eel weekend)	the weekend
romantico (roe-man-teek-oh)	romantic
fantastico (fan-tass-teek-oh)	fantastic
politico (pol-ee-teek-oh)	political
illogico (ee-lodge-eek-oh)	illogical
entusiasta[3] (en-tooze-ee-ast-a)	enthusiastic
Ho (o)	I have
visitato (visit-art-oh)	visited
Ho visitato (o visit-art-oh)	I have visited / I visited / I did visit
Roma (roam-er)	Rome
Napoli (nap-oh-lee)	Naples
Ho visitato Napoli. (o visit-art-oh nap-oh-lee)	I have visited Naples / I visited Naples / I did visit Naples.
passato (pass-art-oh)	spent
Ho passato (o pass-art-oh)	I have spent / I spent / I did spend
Ha (a)	You have
Ha passato (a pass-art-oh)	You have spent / You spent / You did spend
Abbiamo (ab-ee-arm-oh)	We have
Abbiamo passato (ab-ee-arm-oh pass-art-oh)	We have spent / We spent / We did spend
settembre (se-tem-bray)	September
il Natale (eel nat-arl-ay)	Christmas
a Roma (a roam-er)	in Rome

---

3   In everything in life you will find exceptions to the rule and the same is true with these wonderful "ic" and "ical" Word Robberies. Although these conversions work almost all the time, "enthusiastic" is an exception to this technique that I would like you to learn. It's still an easy word to pick up, as it is so similar to the English, but it does not change in the way you would expect it to. I will leave it in the checklists from now on so that you learn it well.

in Italia (een eet-al-yer)	in Italy
in Svizzera (een zvee-tser-er)	in Switzerland
Abbiamo passato il Natale in Svizzera. (ab-ee-arm-oh pass-art-oh eel nat-arl-ay een zvee-tser-er)	We have spent Christmas in Switzerland / We spent Christmas in Switzerland / We did spend Christmas in Switzerland.
Ha passato settembre in Italia. (a pass-art-oh se-tem-bray een eet-al-yer)	You have spent September in Italy / You spent September in Italy / You did spend September in Italy.
e (ay)	and
Era (air-ah)	It was
Era fantastico. (air-ah fan-tass-teek-oh)	It was fantastic.
Il tempo era fantastico. (eel-tem-poe air-ah fan-tass-teek-oh)	The weather was fantastic.
Ho passato il weekend a Roma – e wow, il tempo era fantastico. (o pass-art-oh eel weekend a roam-er ay wow, eel-tem-poe air-ah fan-tass-teek-oh)	I spent the weekend in Rome – and wow, the weather was fantastic.
preparazione (prep-are-atz-ee-oh-nay)	preparation
preparato (pray-par-ato)	prepared
prenotazione (pray-no-tatz-ee-oh-nay)	reservation
prenotato (pray-no-tart-oh)	reserved / booked
ordinato (or-din-art-oh)	ordered
pagato (pag-art-oh)	paid
fatto (fat-oh)	done
il conto (eel kon-toe)	the bill
la cena (la chain-er)	the dinner
il caffè (eel ka-fe)	the coffee
un tavolo (oon tav-oh-loe)	a table
una camera (oon-a cam-air-a)	a room

un taxi (oon taxi)	a taxi
Ho preparato la cena. (o prep-are-art-oh la chain-er)	I have prepared the dinner / I prepared the dinner / I did prepare the dinner.
Ho ordinato il caffè per la cena. (o or-din-art-oh eel ka-fe pair la chain-er)	I have ordered coffee for dinner / I ordered coffee for dinner / I did order coffee for dinner.
Ho prenotato un tavolo per Lei. (o pray-no-tart-oh oon tav-oh-loe pair lay)	I have booked a table for you / I booked a table for you / I did book a table for you.
Lei ha (lay a)	She has
Lei ha prenotato un tavolo per questa sera. (lay a pray no-tart-oh oon tav-oh-loe pair kwest-er sair-er)	She has booked / reserved a table for this evening – She booked / reserved a table for this evening – She did book / reserve a table for this evening.
Lui ha (loo-ee a)	He has
Lui ha prenotato una camera per due persone. (loo-ee a pray-no-tart-oh oon-a cam-air-a pair doo-ay pair-soan-ay)	He has booked / reserved a room for two people – He booked / reserved a room for two people – He did book / reserve a room for two people.
Abbiamo prenotato un taxi per Lei. (ab-ee-arm-oh pray-no-tart oh oon taxi pair lay)	We have booked a taxi for you / We booked a taxi for you / We did book a taxi for you.
Abbiamo pagato il conto. (ab-ee-arm-oh pag-art-oh eel kon-toe)	We paid the bill / We have paid the bill / We did pay the bill.
Che cosa? (ke koe-ser)	What? / What thing?
Che cosa ha preparato? (ke koe-ser a prep-are-art-oh)	What have you prepared? / What did you prepare? (literally "What thing you have prepared?")
Che cosa ha fatto? (ke koe-ser a fat-oh)	What have you done? / What did you do? (literally "What thing you have done?")

Ho prenotato un tavolo, ordinato la cena e poi pagato il conto. Che cosa ha fatto? (o pray-no-tart-oh oon tav-oh-loe, or-din-art-oh la chain-er ey poy pag-art-oh eel kon-toe. ke koe-ser a fat-oh)	I booked a table, ordered dinner and then paid the bill. What did you do?
Ho intenzione di... (o in-ten-tzee-oh-nay dee)	I'm planning to... (literally "I have intention of...")
Ho intenzione di ritornare in Italia a maggio. (o in-ten-tzee-oh-nay dee ri-torn-are-ay een eet-al-yer a madge-oh)	I'm planning to go back to Italy in May.
Ho paura di... (o pow-oo-rer dee)	I'm scared of... (literally "I have fear of...")
Ho paura di ritornare in Italia a settembre. (o pow-oo-rer dee ri-torn-are-ay een eet-al-yer a se-tem-bray)	I'm scared of going back to Italy in September.
Veramente? (ve-ra-men-tay)	Really?
quindi (kwin-dee)	so
ma (mu)	but
Ho voglia di... (o vol-ya dee)	I feel like... / I fancy... (literally "I have want of...")
Sì, ho voglia di ritornare a Roma ma ho paura di volare, quindi ho intenzione di prendere l'Eurostar. (see, o vol-ya dee ri-torn-are-ay a roam-er mu o pow-oo-rer dee vol-are-ay, kwin-dee o in-ten-tzee-oh-nay dee pren-de-rey lay-oo-roe-star)	Yes, I feel like going back to Rome but I'm scared of flying, so I'm planning to take the Eurostar.
Ho voglia di comprare qualcosa questa mattina. (o vol-ya dee com-prar-ay kwal-koe-zer kwest-er mat-een-er	I feel like / fancy buying something this morning.
Lui ha voglia di leggere qualcosa questo pomeriggio. (loo-ee a vol-ya dee ledge-er-ay kwal-koe-zer kwest-oh pom-air-idge-oh)	He feels like / fancies reading something this afternoon.

Loro hanno (lo-roe an-oh)	They have
Loro hanno voglia di mangiare qualcosa questa sera. (lo-roe an-oh vol-ya dee mange-are-ay kwal-koe-zer kwest-er sair-er)	They feel like eating something this evening.
Ho bisogno di... (o beez-on-yoe dee)	I need... (literally "I have need of...")
Ho bisogno di parlare italiano. (o beez-on-yoe dee par-lar-ay eet-al-ee-arn-oh)	I need to speak Italian.
Ho bisogno di un taxi. (o beez-on-yoe dee oon taxi)	I need a taxi.
Ho bisogno di una camera. (o beez-on-yoe dee oon-a cam-air-a)	I need a room.
Ho bisogno di aiuto. (o bisogno di eye-oot-oh)	I need help.
Hai bisogno di aiuto, amico! (eye bisogno di eye-oot-oh am-ee-koe)	You need help, mate!
Ho l'orrore di... (o lo-roar-ay dee)	I can't stand... / I hate... (literally "I have the horror of...")
Ho l'orrore di volare! (o lo-roar-ay dee vol-are-ay)	I can't stand flying! / I hate flying!
Ho l'orrore di abitare con i miei suoceri. (o lo-roar-ay dee ab-it-are-ay kon ee mee-ay soo-o-chair-ee)	I can't stand living with my in-laws / I hate living with my in-laws.
Abbiamo l'orrore di mangiare con i miei genitori. (ab-ee-arm-oh lo-roar-ay dee mange-are-ay kon ee mee-ay jen-ee-tore-ee)	We can't stand eating with my parents / We hate eating with my parents.
Lei ha l'orrore di lavorare qui. (lay a lo-roar-ay dee lavo-or-are-ay kwee)	She can't stand working here / She hates working here.
Ero (air-oh)	I was
solitario (sol-eet-are-ee-oh)	solitary
contrario (kon-trar-ee-oh)	contrary
ordinario (or-deen-are-ee-oh)	ordinary

Ero ordinario. (air-oh or-deen-are-ee-oh)	I was ordinary.
Stavo per... (starve-oh pair)	I was about to... / I was just about to... (literally "I stayed for...")
Stavo per preparare la cena. (starve-oh pair pray-par-are-ay la chain-er)	I was about to prepare the dinner / I was just about to prepare the dinner.
Stavo per pagare il conto. (starve-oh pair pag-are-ay eel kon-toe)	I was about to pay the bill.[4]
Stavo per prenotare un tavolo. (starve-oh pair pray-note-are-ay oon tav-oh-loe)	I was just about to book a table.
Mi ha chiamato. (mee a kee-am-art-oh)	You called me / You did call me / You have called me. (formal)
Mi hai chiamato. (mee eye kee-am-art-oh)	You called me / You did call me / You have called me. (informal)
quando (kwan-doe)	when
Stavo per prenotare un taxi quando mi hai chiamato. Veramente! (starve-oh pair pray-note-are-ay oon taxi kwan-doe mee eye kee-am-art-oh. ve-ra-men-tay)	I was just about to book a taxi when you called me. Really!
Stavo per partire quando il telefono ha squillato. (starve-oh pair part-ear-ray kwan-doe eel tel-off-on-oh a skwee-lar-toe)	I was about to leave when the telephone rang.
Stavo per telefonarti quando hai bussato alla porta. (starve-oh pair tel-ef-own-are-tee kwan-doe eye boos-art-oh al-la port-er)	I was just about to phone you when you knocked at the door. (informal)
Stavo per ordinare un taxi quando ha cominciato a piovere. (starve-oh pair or-din-are-ay oon taxi kwan-doe a kom-in-chart-oh a pee-oh-vair-ay)	I was just about to order a taxi when it started to rain.

---

4 All of the "stavo per..." sentences here can be translated as "I was about to..." or "I was *just* about to...". Sometimes only one translation is given but, in all cases, you could translate it either way.

Okay, time for the other way around. Isn't it strange how translating Italian into English is much easier than translating English into Italian...?

the weekend	il weekend (eel weekend)
romantic	romantico (roe-man-teek-oh)
fantastic	fantastico (fan-tass-teek-oh)
political	politico (pol-ee-teek-oh)
illogical	illogico (ee-lodge-eek-oh)
enthusiastic	entusiasta (en-tooze-ee-ast-a)
I have	Ho (o)
visited	visitato (visit-art-oh)
I have visited / I visited / I did visit	Ho visitato (o visit-art-oh)
Rome	Roma (roam-er)
Naples	Napoli (nap-oh-lee)
I have visited Naples / I visited Naples / I did visit Naples.	Ho visitato Napoli. (o visit-art-oh nap-oh-lee)
spent	passato (pass-art-oh)
I have spent / I spent / I did spend	Ho passato (o pass-art-oh)
You have	Ha (a)
You have spent / You spent / You did spend	Ha passato (a pass-art-oh)
We have	Abbiamo (ab-ee-arm-oh)
We have spent / We spent / We did spend	Abbiamo passato (ab-ee-arm-oh pass-art-oh)
September	settembre (se-tem-bray)
Christmas	il Natale (eel nat-arl-ay)
in Rome	a Roma (a roam-er)
in Italy	in Italia (een eet-al-yer)
in Switzerland	in Svizzera (een zvee-tser-er)
We have spent Christmas in Switzerland / We spent Christmas in Switzerland / We did spend Christmas in Switzerland.	Abbiamo passato il Natale in Svizzera. (ab-ee-arm-oh pass-art-oh eel nat-arl-ay een zvee-tser-er)

You have spent September in Italy / You spent September in Italy / You did spend September in Italy.	Ha passato settembre in Italia. (a pass-art-oh se-tem-bray een eet-al-yer)
and	e (ay)
It was	Era (air-ah)
It was fantastic.	Era fantastico. (air-ah fan-tass-teek-oh)
The weather was fantastic.	Il tempo era fantastico. (eel-tem-poe air-ah fan-tass-teek-oh)
I spent the weekend in Rome – and wow, the weather was fantastic.	Ho passato il weekend a Roma – e wow, il tempo era fantastico. (o pass-art-oh eel weekend a roam-er ay wow, eel-tem-poe air-ah fan-tass-teek-oh)
preparation	preparazione (prep-are-atz-ee-oh-nay)
prepared	preparato (pray-par-ay)
reservation	prenotazione (pray-no-tatz-ee-oh-nay)
reserved / booked	prenotato (pray-no-tart-oh)
ordered	ordinato (or-din-art-oh)
paid	pagato (pag-art-oh)
done	fatto (fat-oh)
the bill	il conto (eel kon-toe)
the dinner	la cena (la chain-er)
the coffee	il caffè (eel ka-fe)
a table	un tavolo (oon tav-oh-loe)
a room	una camera (oon-a cam-air-a)
a taxi	un taxi (oon taxi)
I have prepared the dinner / I prepared the dinner / I did prepare the dinner.	Ho preparato la cena. (o prep-are-art-oh la chain-er)
I have ordered coffee for dinner / I ordered coffee for dinner / I did order coffee for dinner.	Ho ordinato il caffè per la cena. (o or-din-art-oh eel ka-fe pair la chain-er)

I have booked a table for you / I booked a table for you / I did book a table for you.	**Ho prenotato un tavolo per Lei.** (*o pray-no-tart-oh oon tav-oh-loe pair lay*)
She has	**Lei ha** (*lay a*)
She has booked / reserved a table for this evening – She booked / reserved a table for this evening – She did book / reserve a table for this evening.	**Lei ha prenotato un tavolo per questa sera.** (*lay a pray-no-tart-oh oon tav-oh-loe pair kwest-er sair-er*)
He has	**Lui ha** (*loo-ee a*)
He has booked / reserved a room for two people – He booked / reserved a room for two people – He did book / reserve a room for two people.	**Lui ha prenotato una camera per due persone.** (*loo-ee a pray-no-tart-oh oon-a cam-air-a pair doo-ay pair-soan-ay*)
We have booked a taxi for you / We booked a taxi for you / We did book a taxi for you.	**Abbiamo prenotato un taxi per Lei.** (*ab-ee-arm-oh pray-no-tart-oh oon taxi pair lay*)
We paid the bill / We have paid the bill / We did pay the bill.	**Abbiamo pagato il conto.** (*ab-ee-arm-oh pag-art-oh eel kon-toe*)
What? / What thing?	**Che cosa?** (*ke koe-ser*)
What have you prepared? / What did you prepare? (literally "What thing you have prepared?")	**Che cosa ha preparato?** (*ke koe-ser a prep-are-art-oh*)
What have you done? / What did you do? (literally "What thing you have done?")	**Che cosa ha fatto?** (*ke koe-ser a fat-oh*)
I booked a table, ordered dinner and then paid the bill. What did you do?	**Ho prenotato un tavolo, ordinato la cena e poi pagato il conto. Che cosa ha fatto?** (*o pray-no-tart-oh oon tav-oh-loe, or-din-art-oh la chain-er ey poy pag-art-oh eel kon-toe. ke koe-ser a fat-oh*)
I'm planning to...	**Ho intenzione di...** (*o in-ten-tzee-oh-nay dee*)
I'm planning to go back to Italy in May.	**Ho intenzione di ritornare in Italia a maggio.** (*o in-ten-tzee-oh-nay dee ri-torn-are-ay een eet-al-yer a madge-oh*)

I'm scared of...	Ho paura di... (o pow-oo-rer dee)
I'm scared of going back to Italy in September.	Ho paura di ritornare in Italia a settembre. (o pow-oo-rer dee ri-torn-are-ay een eet-al-yer a se-tem-bray)
Really?	Veramente? (ve-ra-men-tay)
so	quindi (kwin-dee)
but	ma (mu)
I feel like... / I fancy... (literally "I have want of...")	Ho voglia di... (o vol-ya dee)
Yes, I feel like / fancy going back to Rome but I'm scared of flying, so I'm planning to take the Eurostar.	Sì, ho voglia di ritornare a Roma ma ho paura di volare, quindi ho intenzione di prendere l'Eurostar. (see, o vol-ya dee ri-torn-are-ay a roam-er mu o pow-oo-rer dee vol-are-ay, kwin-dee o in-ten-tzee-oh-nay dee pren-de-rey lay-oo-roe-star)
I feel like / fancy buying something this morning.	Ho voglia di comprare qualcosa questa mattina. (o vol-ya dee com-prar-ay kwal-koe-zer kwest-er mat-een-er
He feels like / fancies reading something this afternoon.	Lui ha voglia di leggere qualcosa questo pomeriggio. (loo-ee a vol-ya dee ledge-er-ay kwal-koe-zer kwest-oh pom-air-idge-oh)
They have	Loro hanno (lo-roe an-oh)
They feel like / fancy eating something this evening.	Loro hanno voglia di mangiare qualcosa questa sera. (lo-roe an-oh vol-ya dee mange-are-ay kwal-koe-zer kwest-er sair-er)
I need... (literally "I have need of...")	Ho bisogno di... (o beez-on-yoe dee)
I need to speak Italian.	Ho bisogno di parlare italiano. (o beez-on-yoe dee par-lar-ay eet-al-ee-arn-oh)
I need a taxi.	Ho bisogno di un taxi. (o beez-on-yoe dee oon taxi)

I need a room.	**Ho bisogno di una camera.** (*o beez-on-yoe dee oon-a cam-air-a*)
I need help.	**Ho bisogno di aiuto.** (*o bisogno di eye-oot-oh*)
You need help, mate!	**Hai bisogno di aiuto, amico!** (*eye bisogno di eye-oot-oh am-ee-koe*)
I can't stand… / I hate… (literally "I have the horror of…")	**Ho l'orrore di…** (*o lo-roar-ay dee*)
I can't stand flying! / I hate flying!	**Ho l'orrore di volare!** (*o lo-roar-ay dee vol-are-ay*)
I can't stand living with my in-laws / I hate living with my in-laws.	**Ho l'orrore di abitare con i miei suoceri.** (*o lo-roar-ay dee ab-it-are-ay kon ee mee-ay soo-o-chair-ee*)
We can't stand eating with my parents / We hate eating with my parents.	**Abbiamo l'orrore di mangiare con i miei genitori.** (*ab-ee-arm-oh lo-roar-ay dee mange-are-ay kon ee mee-ay jen-ee-tore-ee*)
She can't stand working here / She hates working here.	**Lei ha l'orrore di lavorare qui.** (*lay a lo-roar-ay dee lavo-or-are-ay kwee*)
I was	**Ero** (*air-oh*)
solitary	**solitario** (*sol-eet-are-ee-oh*)
contrary	**contrario** (*kon-trar-ee-oh*)
ordinary	**ordinario** (*or-deen-are-ee-oh*)
I was ordinary.	**Ero ordinario.** (*air-oh or-deen-are-ee-oh*)
I was about to… / I was just about to… (literally "I stayed for…")	**Stavo per…** (*starve-oh pair*)
I was about to prepare the dinner / I was just about to prepare the dinner.	**Stavo per preparare la cena.** (*starve-oh pair pray-par-are-ay la chain-er*)
I was about to pay the bill.	**Stavo per pagare il conto.** (*starve-oh pair pag-are-ay eel kon-toe*)
I was just about to book a table.	**Stavo per prenotare un tavolo.** (*starve-oh pair pray-note-are-ay oon tav-oh-loe*)

You called me / You did call me / You have called me. (formal)	**Mi ha chiamato.** (mee a kee-am-art-oh)
You called me / You did call me / You have called me. (informal)	**Mi hai chiamato.** (mee eye kee-am-art-oh)
when	**quando** (kwan-doe)
I was just about to book a taxi when you called me. Really!	**Stavo per prenotare un taxi quando mi hai chiamato. Veramente!** (starve-oh pair pray-note-are-ay oon taxi kwan-doe mee eye kee-am-art-oh. ve-ra-men-tay)
I was about to leave when the telephone rang.	**Stavo per partire quando il telefono ha squillato.** (starve-oh pair part-ear-ray kwan-doe eel tel-off-on-oh a skwee-lar-toe
I was just about to phone you when you knocked at the door. (informal)	**Stavo per telefonarti quando hai bussato alla porta.** (starve-oh pair tel-ef-own-are-tee kwan-doe eye boos-art-oh al-la port-er)
I was just about to order a taxi when it started to rain.	**Stavo per ordinare un taxi quando ha cominciato a piovere.** (starve-oh pair or-din-are-ay oon taxi kwan-doe a kom-in-chart-oh a pee-oh-vair-ay)

That's it. Go and take your well-deserved break!

Forget what you were taught at school!

Many of us were told at school that we did not have an aptitude for languages, that we didn't have a "knack" or a "gift" for them.

Well, if this applies to you, then please let me assure you that this is all absolute nonsense! If you are able to read these words in front of you then this demonstrates that you've been able to learn English. If you can learn one language, then your brain is just as capable of learning another – it simply needs to be approached in the right way.

In fact, if you've got as far as Chapter 5, it should already be obvious to you that you are quite capable of learning a foreign language when it's taught in the right way. The secret to success for you will be choosing the right materials once you've finished with this book (more on that later).

CHAPTER 6 (1)

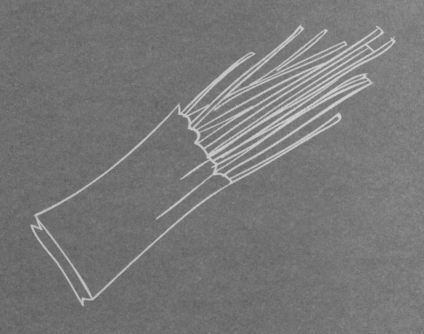

I'm sorry, I was in the middle of preparing dinner when you arrived, so I was a bit distracted. (part 1)

> I'm sorry, I was in the middle of preparing dinner when you arrived, so I was a bit distracted.

Isn't it annoying when people turn up just as you're in the middle of something? And how much worse is it that you then need to apologise to them for ignoring them when they do?

Still, that's life, so you'd better get ready to deal with it in Italian!

So, remind me, how would you say "I have reserved", "I reserved", "I did reserve" in Italian?

Ho prenotato
(o pray-no-tart-oh)

And how would you say "I have prepared," "I prepared", "I did prepare"?

Ho preparato
(o prep-are-art-oh)

How about "I have paid", "I paid", "I did pay"?

Ho pagato
(o pag-art-oh)

And how would you say "you have paid", "you paid", "you did pay" (formal)?

Ha pagato
(a pag-art-oh)

And what about "you have paid", "you paid", "you did pay" (informal)?

Hai pagato
(eye pag-art-oh)

As you learnt early on, in Italian you get three English past tenses for the price of one in Italian.

This means that by simply knowing how to say "I have...", "you have...", "we have...", and so on you can express all three of these tenses, which is wonderful news for English speakers studying Italian.

However, it isn't entirely good news...

Although what I have said above is true in almost every instance in Italian, there is a set of words that work somewhat differently. These are words that, shall we say, come and go in a different way to the others. Let me explain.

Important comings and goings!

You already know that, when you want to use the past tense in Italian, you use "have".

So, to say "I reserved" in Italian you'll simply say "I *have* reserved", to say "you prepared" you'll say "you *have* prepared". You should be very used to this by now.

However, when you are talking about your comings and goings in Italian, you cannot use "have" to make the past tense.

So, for instance:

To say "I went" in Italian you will **not** say "I have gone"!

To say "I came" in Italian you will **not** say "I have come"!

To say "I left" in Italian (a type of going, I'm sure you'll agree) you will **not** say "I have left"!

And to say "I arrived" in Italian (a type of coming, I'm sure you'll also agree) you will **not** say "I have arrived"!

No, you cannot use "have" with these words, instead, strange as it sounds, you will use "am".

So, for example:

To say "I went" you will say "I **am** gone"!

To say "I came" you will say "I **am** come"!

To say "I left" you will say "I **am** left"!

To say "I arrived" you will say "I **am** arrived"!

This sounds odd but, as I'll show you, it's something that's actually very easy to do. It's just an unfamiliar idea to us as English speakers, that's all!

Let me show you how this works in practice.

Let's imagine for a moment that I, the author, Paul Noble, have just arrived somewhere. And perhaps I decide to ring someone to tell them, very simply, that "I have arrived".

So, to begin with, the word I will use for "arrived" in Italian would be:

arrivato
(a-reev-art-oh)

Now, "I am" in Italian is:

Sono
(son-oh)

So, how would you say "I am arrived"?

Sono arrivato.
(son-oh a-reev-art-oh)

And this means "I arrived", "I have arrived" and "I did arrive".

Notice that "I have" (ho) has not been used because you will not use "have" when you are talking about your comings and goings.

Let's just check this again to make sure you have fully understood.

What is "I am" in Italian?

Sono
(son-oh)

And what is the word you have learnt for "arrived"?

arrivato
(a-reev-art-oh)

How would you say "I arrived"?

Sono arrivato.
(son-oh a-reev-art-oh)

How about "I did arrive"?

Sono arrivato.
(son-oh a-reev-art-oh)

And "I have arrived"?

Sono arrivato.
(son-oh a-reev-art-oh)

Just as before, these are all the same in Italian, the only difference is that because arriving is a type of coming and going, you're not allowed to use "have" with it.

Also before I forget, I should mention that there's something else to be aware of, something which affects words such as "arrived" in Italian. This is something that I like to call "The Mario-Maria Rule".

The Mario-Maria Rule

You may well be thinking, "what on earth is this?"

Well, the names Mario and Maria tell us something very interesting about Italian.

They show us that male or masculine things in the Italian language tend to end with an "o" – like the name "Mario" – but that female or feminine things tend to end with an "a" – like the name "Maria".

In Italian, however, this affects more than just people's names. It also affects, for instance, the words that we use to describe those people.

For example, if you want to say "Mario is romantic" in Italian, you will say:

Mario è romantico.
(ma-ree-oh ay roe-man-teek-oh)

You will notice that there is an "o" on the end of both "Mario" and the Italian word for "romantic" (romantico).

With this in mind, can you guess how you would say "Maria is romantic" in Italian?

Maria è romantica.
(ma-ree-ah ay roe-man-teek-a)

So, here we can see that the word for "romantic" changes depending on whether it is describing someone male (masculine) or female (feminine). For masculine, we put an "o" on the end of the describing word and for feminine we put an "a" at the end. This is the Mario-Maria Rule in action.

And the Mario-Maria Rule is also something that is used in Italian whenever you create the past tense using "am". Let's look at an example to make this easier to understand.

As I've already said, if I, the author (and I'm a guy) wanted to say "I have arrived", I would say:

Sono arrivato.
(son-oh a-reev-art-oh)

But if a woman said the same thing, she would instead say:

Sono arrivata.
(son-oh a-reev-art-a)

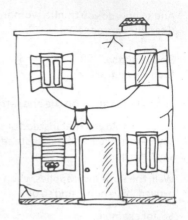

So you can see how, although it is "arrivato" for a man who has arrived, it is by contrast "arrivata" for a woman, with an "**a**" on the end – just like the name Mario is for a man but Maria is for a woman.

As I've said though, this only applies when you are talking about your comings and goings, that is, when you use "am" instead of "have" to make the past tense.

When you use "have" to make the past tense (which is what you normally do), the spelling doesn't change; take a look:

| I have reserved (said by a man) | *Ho prenotato* |
| | *(o pray-no-tart-oh)* |

| I have reserved (said by a woman) | *Ho prenotato* |
| | *(o pray-no-tart-oh)* |

You see? They are the same – and they never change!

However, when a man or woman is talking about coming or going or arriving or leaving, then it does change.

"Gone" referring to a man in Italian is:

andato
(and-art-oh)

So, how would a man say "I have gone", "I went", "I did go" (literally "I am gone")?

Sono andato.
(son-oh and-art-oh)

And so how do you think a woman would say "I have gone", "I went", "I did go" (literally "I am gone")?

Sono andata.
(son-oh and-art-a)

Look, there's an "a" on the end rather than an "o"!

Now, I've told you that instead of saying "I have arrived" in Italian, you will literally say "I am arrived" and that instead of saying "I have gone" in Italian, you'll literally say "I am gone."

Well, the same logic applies when you're saying "he", "she", "you", "we", "they" went, arrived, have gone , and so on.

So, for example:

If you want to say "he has gone" you'll say literally "he *is* gone".
If you want to say "she has gone", you'll literally say "she *is* gone".
If you want to say "you have gone" you'll literally say "you *are* gone".

"You are" (formal) in Italian is:

È
(ay)

So, how do you think you would say "you have gone" (formal) when you're talking **to a man**?

È andato.
(ay and-art-oh)

And how do you think you would say it when you're talking **to a woman**?

È andata.
(ay and-art-a)

And how would say "you have arrived", "you arrrived", "you did arrive" (formal) when talking **to a man**?

È arrivato.
(ay a-reev-art-oh)

And how would you say it **to a woman**?

È arrivata.
(ay a-reev-art-a)

So, this change applies both when someone is saying it about themselves or when you are saying it about someone else. It changes based on the gender of the person being described.

"You are" (informal) in Italian is:

Sei
(say)

How would you say to a woman "you have arrived", "you arrived", "you did arrive" (informal)?

Sei arrivata.
(say a-reev-art-a)

And how would you say the same thing to a man?

Sei arrivato.
(say a-reev-art-oh)

Okay, let's just leave it at that for the moment. When you're ready, you can go on to the next chapter and you can complete the sentence. But before you do that, feel free to read through this chapter a few times, practising the sentence-building. That will help you feel comfortable with this aspect of Italian.

In case it's helpful, I'm also going to provide you with a quick summary of what you really need to grasp from this chapter. So, the three key points that I want you to take from it are:

1. The Mario-Maria Rule only affects words to do with your comings and goings (go, come, arrive, leave, and so on). For other words, like when you want to say you've booked or paid for or ordered something, just use "have" to make the past tense (like you did at the start of this book).

2. When you are talking about your comings and goings, however, you do need to use "am" or "is" or "are" when you want to say that someone has arrived, gone, come or left. So, you say "I *am* arrived" not "I *have* arrived", and you say "you *are* gone" not "you *have* gone". I know it seems weird – just try to accept it!

3. The words for "arrived", "went", "came" or "left" in Italian will have an "o" at the end of them when they are said about someone male and an "a" at the end of them when they are said about someone female – just like with the names Mario and Maria.

That's it. If you've more or less got those points, then you're ready to move on.

CHAPTER 6 (2)

I'm sorry, I was in the middle of preparing dinner when you arrived, so I was a bit distracted. (part 2)

> *I'm sorry, I was in the middle of preparing dinner when you arrived, so I was a bit distracted.*

Alright, now that you're aware of the Mario-Maria Rule, let's get back to building this sentence.

So again, how would you say "I was about to..." (literally "I stayed for...") in Italian?

Stavo per...
(starve-oh pair)

And how would you say "I was about to book a taxi"?

Stavo per prenotare un taxi.
(starve-oh pair pray-note-are-ay oon taxi)

How about "I was about to pay the bill"?

Stavo per pagare il conto.
(starve-oh pair pag-are-ay eel kon-toe)

And "I was about to prepare the dinner"?

Stavo per preparare la cena.
(starve-oh pair pray-par-are-ay la chain-er)

You should now be quite familiar with the phrase "I was about to..." and it's certainly very useful.

There is another similarly structured phrase in Italian, which is equally useful and which means "I was in the middle of..."

Now, to say, for instance, "I was in the middle of preparing the dinner" in Italian, you will literally say "I stayed preparing the dinner."

Now, the "I stayed" part you already know. What is "I stayed"?

stavo
(starve-oh)

To say the "preparing" bit, you will first of all take the Italian word for "to prepare". What is "to prepare" in Italian?

preparare
(pray-par-are-ay)

You will then chop the "are" off at the end. Do that now. What are you left with?

prepar
(pray-par)

Now, to make this "prepar" into "preparing", instead of adding an "ing" onto the end as we would in English, in Italian you will add an "ando".

So, do this now, add "ando" onto the end of "prepar" and tell me, what will "preparing" be in Italian?

preparando
(pray-par-and-oh)

And so how will you say "I was in the middle of preparing" (literally "I stayed preparing")?

Stavo preparando
(starve-oh pray-par-and-oh)

How would you say "I was in the middle of preparing the dinner" (literally "I stayed preparing the dinner")?

Stavo preparando la cena.
(starve-oh pray-par-ay la chain-er)

What is "to pay"?

pagare
(pag-are-ay)

To turn this into "paying", you will again cut the "are" off the end of the word and add "ando" in its place.

So, what will "paying" be in Italian?

pagando
(pag-and-oh)

So how would you say "I was in the middle of paying" (literally "I stayed paying")?

Stavo pagando.
(starve-oh pag-and-oh)

And how about "I was in the middle of paying the bill"?

Stavo pagando il conto.
(starve-oh pag-and-oh eel kon-toe)

What is "to reserve" or "to book"?

prenotare
(pray-note-are-ay)

And so how would you say "I was in the middle of booking a taxi"?

Stavo prenotando un taxi.
(starve-oh pray-note-and-oh oon taxi)

What is "to eat?"

mangiare
(mange-are-ay)

So, how would you say "I was in the middle of eating" (literally "I stayed eating")?

Stavo mangiando.
(starve-oh mange-and-oh)

And again, how would a man say "I have arrived", "I arrived", "I did arrive" in Italian (literally "I am arrived")?

Sono arrivato.
(son-oh a-reev-art-oh)

What about a woman?

Sono arrivata.
(son-oh a-reev-art-a)

And how would you say to a man (formal) "you have arrived", "you arrived", "you did arrive"?

È arrivato.
(ay a-reev-art-oh)

How about to a woman (formal) "you have arrived", "you arrived", "you did arrive"?

È arrivata.
(ay a-reev-art-a)

And what about to a woman (informal) "you have arrived", "you arrived", "you did arrive"?

Sei arrivata.
(say a-reev-art-a)

And how would you say the same to a man (informal) "you have arrived", "you arrived", "you did arrive"?

Sei arrivato.
(say a-reev-art-oh)

What is the word for "when" in Italian?

quando
(kwan-doe)

So, how would you say "...when you arrived" (informal)?

...quando sei arrivato / arrivata
(kwan-doe say a-reev-art-oh / a-reev-art-a)

And again, how would you say "I was in the middle of..."?

Stavo...
(starve-oh)

What about "I was in the middle of preparing the dinner"?

Stavo preparando la cena.
(starve-oh pray-par-and-oh la chain-er)

And "I was in the middle of eating"?

Stavo mangiando.
(starve-oh mange-and-oh)

So how would you say "I was in the middle of eating when you arrived" (informal)?

Stavo mangiando quando sei arrivato / arrivata.
(starve-oh mange-and-oh kwan-doe say a-reev-art-oh / a-reev-art-a)

And "I was in the middle of preparing the dinner when you arrived" (informal)?

Stavo preparando la cena quando sei arrivato / arrivata.
(starve-oh pray-par-and-oh la chain-er kwan-doe say a-reev-art-oh / a-reev-art-a)

To say "I'm sorry" in Italian, you will express the idea by saying that it displeases you. Literally you will say "me displeases", which is:

mi dispiace
(mee dis-pee-arch-ey)

So how would you say "I'm sorry, I was in the middle of preparing the dinner when you arrived" (informal)?

Mi dispiace, stavo preparando la cena quando sei arrivato / arrivata.
(mee dis-pee-arch-ey, starve-oh pray-par-and-oh la chain-er kwan-doe say a-reev-art-oh / a-reev-art-a)

And how would you say "I'm sorry, I was in the middle of eating when you arrived" (informal)?

Mi dispiace, stavo mangiando quando sei arrivato / arrivata.
(mee dis-pee-arch-ey, starve-oh mange-and-oh kwan-doe say a-reev-art-oh / a-reev-art-a)

Now, once more, just on its own, what is "I was" in Italian?

Ero
(air-oh)

How would you say "I was romantic"?

Ero romantico.
(air-oh roe-man-teek-oh)

And once more, what is the word for "so" in Italian?

quindi
(kwin-dee)

It's worth pointing out that in English we actually use "so" to mean more than one thing. For instance, we can say "I liked the jacket, so I bought it" or "I'm not happy here, so I'm leaving." It's sort of a less formal way of saying "therefore" – "I like the jacket, therefore I bought it", "I'm not happy here, therefore I'm leaving." (It would, of course, sound a bit strange to actually use "therefore" in these situations because it's somewhat formal – but the meaning is essentially the same).

Anyway, this is the type of "so" that you have been using "quindi" to express in Italian, the "so" that is a less formal way of saying "therefore". This is the kind of "so" you would use in the examples I've just given, or to say something like "I'm tired, so I'm going to bed."

There is, however, another way in which we use "so" in English. This "so" is used, for instance, when we say "I was so happy", "I was so excited", "he's so romantic". This "so" clearly isn't the same as the "therefore" we have been using so far. It's meaning is more like "very" or "extremely".

The word for this type of "so" in Italian is:

così
(koh-zee)

So, how would you say "I was so romantic"?

Ero così romantico.
(air-oh koh-zee roe-man-teek-oh)

How about "I was so illogical"?

Ero così illogico.
(air-oh koh-zee ee-lodge-eek-oh)

"I was so ordinary"?

Ero così ordinario.
(air-oh koh-zee or-deen-are-ee-oh)

"Distracted" in Italian is:

distratto / distratta[5]
(dee-stra-toe / dee-stra-ta)

So, how would you say "I was so distracted"?

Ero così distratto / distratta.
(air-oh dee-stra-toe / dee-stra-ta)

And now let's take away the "so" and say simply "I was distracted?"

Ero distratto / distratta.
(air-oh dee-stra-toe / dee-stra-ta)

---

[5] Notice again the Mario-Maria Rule in action. So, we use "distratto" to describe someone male and "distratta" to describe someone female.

"A bit" or "a little" in Italian is:

un po'
(*oon po*)

So, how would you say "I was a bit distracted", "I was a little distracted"?

Ero un po' distratto / distratta.
(air-oh oon po dee-stra-toe / dee-stra-ta)

Now again, what was "so" in the sense of "extremely" or "very" in Italian?

così
(koh-zee)

And what was "so" meaning "therefore"?

quindi
(kwin-dee)

So, how would you say "...so I was a bit distracted", meaning "...therefore I was a little distracted"?

...quindi ero un po' distratto / distratta
(kwin-dee air-oh oon po dee-stra-toe / dee-stra-ta)

And again, how would you say "I'm sorry" (literally "me displeases")?

Mi dispiace
(mee dis-pee-arch-ey)

And what was "I was in the middle of eating" (literally "I stayed eating")?

Stavo mangiando
(starve-oh mange-and-oh)

Okay, how would you say "I'm sorry, I was in the middle of eating when you arrived" (informal) – (literally "Me displeases, I stayed eating when you arrived")?

Mi dispiace, stavo mangiando quando sei arrivato / arrivata.
(mee dis-pee-arch-ey, starve-oh mange-and-oh kwan-doe say a-reev-art-oh / a-reev-art-a)

What about, "I'm sorry, I was in the middle of preparing dinner when you arrived" (informal)?

Mi dispiace, stavo preparando la cena quando sei arrivato / arrivata.
(mee dis-pee-arch-ey, starve-oh pray-par-and-oh la chain-er kwan-doe say a-reev-art-oh / a-reev-art-a)

Finally, let's imagine you had been preparing a dinner for some special guests when your friend came over to see you. To explain your mood you wanted to say "I'm sorry, I was in the middle of preparing dinner when you arrived, so I was a bit distracted." (informal):

Mi dispiace, stavo preparando la cena quando sei arrivato / arrivata, quindi ero un po' distratto / distratta.
(mee dis-pee-arch-ey, starve-oh pray-par-ando la chain-er kwan-doe say a-reev-art-oh / a-reev-art-a, kwin-dee air-oh oon po dee-stra-toe / dee-stra-ta)

Well done with that! Again, take your time practising that last sentence until you feel confident constructing it. There's never a need to rush on to the next section until you feel you have properly finished with the previous one.

Sixth chapter, six new building blocks:

cenando
(chen-an-doe)
having dinner*1

studiando
(stood-ee-and-oh)
studying

**quando la tua
lettera è arrivata**
(kwan-doe la too-a let-air-a ay a-reev-art-a)
when your letter arrived*2

**quando mi hai
telefonato**
(kwan-doe mee eye tay-lay-fone-art-oh)
when you phoned me

cucinando
(koo-cheen-an-doe)
cooking*3

**quando mia madre
è arrivata**
(kwan-doe mee-a mard-re ay a-reev-art-a)
when my mother arrived*4

*1 literally "dining/dinner-ing"

*2 literally "when your letter is arrived"

*3 literally "kitchen-ing"

*4 literally "when my mother is arrived"

Now build me some sentences, please!

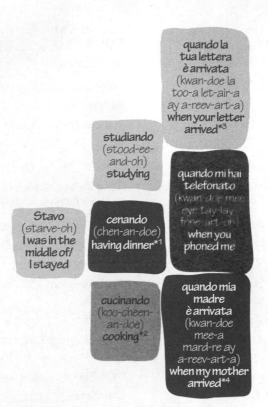

quando la tua lettera è arrivata
(kwan-doe la too-a let-air-a ay a-reev-art-a)
when your letter arrived*3

studiando
(stood-ee-and-oh)
studying

quando mi hai telefonato
(kwan-doe mee eye tay-lay fone-art-oh)
when you phoned me

Stavo
(starve-oh)
I was in the middle of/ I stayed

cenando
(chen-an-doe)
having dinner*1

cucinando
(koo-cheen-an-doe)
cooking*2

quando mia madre è arrivata
(kwan-doe mee-a mard-re ay a-reev-art-a)
when my mother arrived*4

*1 literally "dining/dinner-ing"

*2 literally "kitchen-ing"

*3 literally "when your letter is arrived"

*4 literally "when my mother is arrived"

Checklist 6

Checklist number 6, take your time and enjoy it (if you can)!

il weekend (eel weekend)	**the weekend**
romantico (roe-man-teek-oh)	**romantic**
fantastico (fan-tass-teek-oh)	**fantastic**
politico (pol-ee-teek-oh)	**political**

illogico (ee-lodge-eek-oh)	illogical
entusiasta[6] (en-tooze-ee-ast-a)	enthusiastic
Ho (o)	I have
visitato (visit-art-oh)	visited
Ho visitato (o visit-art-oh)	I have visited / I visited / I did visit
Roma (roam-er)	Rome
Napoli (nap-oh-lee)	Naples
Ho visitato Napoli. (o visit-art-oh nap-oh-lee)	I have visited Naples / I visited Naples / I did visit Naples.
passato (pass-art-oh)	spent
Ho passato (o pass-art-oh)	I have spent / I spent / I did spend
Ha (a)	You have
Ha passato (a pass-art-oh)	You have spent / You spent / You did spend
Abbiamo (ab-ee-arm-oh)	We have
Abbiamo passato (ab-ee-arm-oh pass-art-oh)	We have spent / We spent / We did spend
settembre (se-tem-bray)	September
il Natale (eel nat-arl-ay)	Christmas
a Roma (a roam-er)	in Rome
in Italia (een eet-al-yer)	in Italy
in Svizzera (een zvee-tser-er)	in Switzerland
Abbiamo passato il Natale in Svizzera. (ab-ee-arm-oh pass-art-oh eel nat-arl-ay een zvee-tser-er)	We have spent Christmas in Switzerland / We spent Christmas in Switzerland / We did spend Christmas in Switzerland.
Ha passato settembre in Italia. (a pass-art-oh se-tem-bray een eet-al-yer)	You have spent September in Italy / You spent September in Italy / You did spend September in Italy.
e (ay)	and
Era (air-ah)	It was

---

6   Something interesting to note about "entusiasta" is that it stays exactly the same, with an "a" on the end, irrespective of whether the person being described is male or female.

Era fantastico. (air-ah fan-tass-teek-oh)	It was fantastic.
Il tempo era fantastico. (eel-tem-poe air-ah fan-tass-teek-oh)	The weather was fantastic.
Ho passato il weekend a Roma – e wow, il tempo era fantastico. (o pass-art-oh eel weekend a roam-er ay wow, eel-tem-poe air-ah fan-tass-teek-oh)	I spent the weekend in Rome – and wow, the weather was fantastic.
preparazione (prep-are-atz-ee-oh-nay)	preparation
preparato (pray-par-ato)	prepared
prenotazione (pray-no-tatz-ee-oh-nay)	reservation
prenotato (pray-no-tart-oh)	reserved / booked
ordinato (or-din-art-oh)	ordered
pagato (pag-art-oh)	paid
fatto (fat-oh)	done
il conto (eel kon-toe)	the bill
la cena (la chain-er)	the dinner
il caffè (eel ka-fe)	the coffee
un tavolo (oon tav-oh-loe)	a table
una camera (oon-a cam-air-a)	a room
un taxi (oon taxi)	a taxi
Ho preparato la cena. (o prep-are-art-oh la chain-er)	I have prepared the dinner / I prepared the dinner / I did prepare the dinner.
Ho ordinato il caffè per la cena. (o or-din-art-oh eel ka-fe pair la chain-er)	I have ordered coffee for dinner / I ordered coffee for dinner / I did order coffee for dinner.
Ho prenotato un tavolo per Lei. (o pray-no-tart-oh oon tav-oh-loe pair lay)	I have booked a table for you / I booked a table for you / I did book a table for you.
Lei ha (lay a)	She has

Lei ha prenotato un tavolo per questa sera. (lay a pray-no-tart-oh oon tav-oh-loe pair kwest-er sair-er)	She has booked / reserved a table for this evening – She booked / reserved a table for this evening – She did book / reserve a table for this evening.
Lui ha (loo-ee a)	He has
Lui ha prenotato una camera per due persone. (loo-ee a pray-no-tart-oh oon-a cam-air-a pair doo-ay pair-soan-ay)	He has booked / reserved a room for two people – He booked / reserved a room for two people – He did book / reserve a room for two people.
Abbiamo prenotato un taxi per Lei. (ab-ee-arm-oh pray-no-tart-oh oon taxi pair lay)	We have booked a taxi for you / We booked a taxi for you / We did book a taxi for you.
Abbiamo pagato il conto. (ab-ee-arm-oh pag-art-oh eel kon-toe)	We paid the bill / We have paid the bill / We did pay the bill.
Che cosa? (ke koe-ser)	What? / What thing?
Che cosa ha preparato? (ke koe-ser a prep-are-art-oh)	What have you prepared? / What did you prepare? (literally "What thing you have prepared?")
Che cosa ha fatto? (ke koe-ser a fat-oh)	What have you done? / What did you do? (literally "What thing you have done?")
Ho prenotato un tavolo, ordinato la cena e poi pagato il conto. Che cosa ha fatto? (o pray-no-tart-oh oon tav-oh-loe, or-din-art-oh la chain-er ey poy pag-art-oh eel kon-toe. ke koe-ser a fat-oh)	I booked a table, ordered dinner and then paid the bill. What did you do?
Ho intenzione di… (o in-ten-tzee-oh-nay dee)	I'm planning to… (Literally "I have intention of…")
Ho intenzione di ritornare in Italia a maggio. (o in-ten-tzee-oh-nay dee ri-torn-are-ay een eet-al-yer a madge-oh)	I'm planning to go back to Italy in May.
Ho paura di… (o pow-oo-rer dee)	I'm scared of… (literally "I have fear of…")

Ho paura di ritornare in Italia a settembre. (*o pow-oo-rer dee ri-torn-are-ay een eet-al-yer a se-tem-bray*)	I'm scared of going back to Italy in September.
Veramente? (*ve-ra-men-tay*)	Really?
quindi (*kwin-dee*)	so (therefore)
ma (*mu*)	but
Ho voglia di… (*o vol-ya dee*)	I feel like… / I fancy… (literally "I have want of…")
Sì, ho voglia di ritornare a Roma ma ho paura di volare, quindi ho intenzione di prendere l'Eurostar. (*see, o vol-ya dee ri-torn-are-ay a roam-er mu o pow-oo rer dee vol-are-ay, kwin-dee o in-ten-tzee-oh-nay dee pren-de-rey lay-oo-roe-star*)	Yes, I feel like going back to Rome but I'm scared of flying, so I'm planning to take the Eurostar.
Ho voglia di comprare qualcosa questa mattina. (*o vol-ya dee com-prar-ay kwal-koe-zer kwest-er mat-een-er*)	I feel like / fancy buying something this morning.
Lui ha voglia di leggere qualcosa questo pomeriggio. (*loo-ee a vol-ya dee ledge-er-ay kwal-koe-zer kwest-oh pom-air-idge-oh*)	He feels like / fancies reading something this afternoon.
Loro hanno (*lo-roe an-oh*)	They have
Loro hanno voglia di mangiare qualcosa questa sera. (*lo-roe an-oh vol-ya dee mange-are-ay kwal-koe-zer kwest-er sair-er*)	They feel like eating something this evening.
Ho bisogno di… (*o beez-on-yoe dee*)	I need… (literally "I have need of…")
Ho bisogno di parlare italiano. (*o beez-on-yoe dee par-lar-ay eet-al-ee-arn-oh*)	I need to speak Italian.
Ho bisogno di un taxi. (*o beez-on-yoe dee oon taxi*)	I need a taxi.
Ho bisogno di una camera. (*o beez-on-yoe dee oon-a cam-air-a*)	I need a room.

Ho bisogno di aiuto. (o bisogno di eye-oot-oh)	I need help.
Hai bisogno di aiuto, amico! (eye bisogno di eye-oot-oh am-ee-koe)	You need help, mate!
Ho l'orrore di... (o lo-roar-ay dee)	I can't stand... / I hate... (literally "I have the horror of...")
Ho l'orrore di volare! (o lo-roar-ay dee vol-are-ay)	I can't stand flying! / I hate flying!
Ho l'orrore di abitare con i miei suoceri. (o lo-roar-ay dee ab-it-are-ay kon ee mee-ay soo-o-chair-ee)	I can't stand living with my in-laws / I hate living with my in-laws.
Abbiamo l'orrore di mangiare con i miei genitori. (ab-ee-arm-oh lo-roar-ay dee mange-are-ay kon ee mee-ay jen-ee-tore-ee)	We can't stand eating with my parents / We hate eating with my parents.
Lei ha l'orrore di lavorare qui. (lay a lo-roar-ay dee lavo-or-are-ay kwee)	She can't stand working here / She hates working here.
Ero (air-oh)	I was
solitario (sol-eet-are-ee-oh)	solitary
contrario (kon-trar-ee-oh)	contrary
ordinario (or-deen-are-ee-oh)	ordinary
Ero ordinario. (air-oh or-deen-are-ee-oh)	I was ordinary.
Stavo per... (starve-oh pair)	I was about to... / I was just about to... (literally "I stayed for...")
Stavo per preparare la cena. (starve-oh pair pray-par-are-ay la chain-er)	I was about to prepare the dinner / I was just about to prepare the dinner.
Stavo per pagare il conto. (starve-oh pair pag-are-ay eel kon-toe)	I was about to pay the bill.
Stavo per prenotare un tavolo. (starve-oh pair pray-note-are-ay oon tav-oh-loe)	I was just about to book a table.
Mi ha chiamato. (mee a kee-am-art-oh)	You called me / You did call me / You have called me. (formal)

Mi hai chiamato. (mee eye kee-am-art-oh)	You called me / You did call me / You have called me. (informal)
quando (kwan-doe)	when
Stavo per prenotare un taxi quando mi hai chiamato. Veramente! (starve-oh pair pray-note-are-ay oon taxi kwan-doe mee eye kee-am-art-oh. ve-ra-men-tay)	I was just about to book a taxi when you called me. Really!
Stavo per partire quando il telefono ha squillato. (starve-oh pair part-ear-ray kwan-doe eel tel-off-on-oh a skwee-lar-toe)	I was about to leave when the telephone rang.
Stavo per telefonarti quando hai bussato alla porta. (starve-oh pair tel-ef-own-are-tee kwan-doe eye boos-art-oh al-la port-er)	I was just about to phone you when you knocked at the door. (informal)
Stavo per ordinare un taxi quando ha cominciato a piovere. (starve-oh pair or-din-are-ay oon taxi kwan-doe a kom-in-chart-oh a pee-oh-vair-ay)	I was just about to order a taxi when it started to rain.
così (koh-see)	so (extremely, very)
Ero così romantico. (air-oh koh-zee roe-man-teek-oh)	I was so romantic.
Ero così illogico. (air-oh koh-zee ee-lodge-eek-oh)	I was so illogical.
è (ay)	is
Mario è romantico. (ma-ree-oh ay roe-man-teek-oh)	Mario is romantic.
Maria è romantica. (ma-ree-ah ay roe-man-teek-a)	Maria is romantic.
Sono (son-oh)	I am
arrivato / arrivata (a-reev-art-oh / a-reev-art-a)	arrived
Sono arrivato. (son-oh a-reev-art-oh)	I have arrived / I arrived / I did arrive. (said by a man / boy)
Sono arrivata. (son-oh a-reev-art-a)	I have arrived / I arrived / I did arrive. (said by a woman / girl)

andato / andata (and-art-oh / and-art-a)	gone
Sono andato. (son-oh and-art-oh)	I have gone / I went / I did go. (said by a man / boy)
Sono andata. (son-oh and-art-oh)	I have gone / I went / I did go. (said by a woman / girl)
È (ay)	You are (formal)
È andato. (ay and-art-oh)	You have gone / you went / you did go. (said to a man / boy) – (formal)
È andata. (ay and-art-oh)	You have gone / you went / you did go. (said to a woman / girl) – (formal)
È arrivato. (ay a-reev-art-oh)	You have arrived / you arrived / you did arrive. (said to a man / boy) – (formal)
È arrivata. (ay a-reev-art-a)	You have arrived / you arrived / you did arrive. (said to a woman / girl) – (formal)
Sei (say)	You are (informal)
Sei arrivato. (say a-reev-art-oh)	You have arrived / you arrived / you did arrive. (said to a man / boy) – (informal)
Sei arrivata. (say a-reev-art-a)	You have arrived / you arrived / you did arrive. (said to a woman / girl) – (informal)
Mi dispiace. (mee dis-pee-arch-ey)	I'm sorry.
un po' (oon po)	a little / a bit
Ero un po' distratto / distratta. (air-oh oon po dee-stra-toe / dee-stra-ta)	I was a little distracted.
Mi dispiace, stavo mangiando quando sei arrivato / arrivata. (mee dis-pee-arch-ey, starve-oh mange-and-oh kwan-doe say a-reev-art-oh / a-reev-art-a)	I'm sorry, I was in the middle of eating when you arrived. (informal)

Mi dispiace, stavo preparando la cena quando sei arrivato / arrivata, quindi ero un po' distratto / distratta. (mee dis-pee-arch-ey, starve-oh pray-par-ay la chain-er kwan-doe say a-reev-art-oh / a-reev-art-a kwin-dee air-oh oon po dee-stra-toe / dee-stra-ta)	I'm sorry, I was in the middle of preparing dinner when you arrived, so I was a bit distracted. (informal)
Stavo studiando quando mia madre è arrivata. (starve-oh stood-ee-and-oh kwan-doe mee-a mard-re ay a-reev-art-a)	I was in the middle of studying when my mother arrived.
Stavo cucinando quando mi hai telefonato. (starve-oh koo-cheen-an-doe kwan-doe mee eye tay-lay-fone-art-oh)	I was in the middle of cooking when you phoned me.
Stavo cenando quando la tua e-mail è arrivata. (starve-oh chen-an-deo kwan-doe la too-a ee-mail ay a-reev-art-a)	I was in the middle of having dinner when your email arrived.

Now enjoy yourself doing it the other way around.

Twice the fun for half the effort... erm... kind of.

the weekend	il weekend (eel weekend)
romantic	romantico (roe-man-teek-oh)
fantastic	fantastico (fan-tass-teek-oh)
political	politico (pol-ee-teek-oh)
illogical	illogico (ee-lodge-eek-oh)
enthusiastic	entusiasta (en-tooze-ee-ast-a)
I have	Ho (o)
visited	visitato (visit-art-oh)
I have visited / I visited / I did visit	Ho visitato (o visit-art-oh)
Rome	Roma (roam-er)

Naples	Napoli (nap-oh-lee)
I have visited Naples / I visited Naples / I did visit Naples.	Ho visitato Napoli. (o visit-art-oh nap-oh-lee)
spent	passato (pass-art-oh)
I have spent / I spent / I did spend	Ho passato (o pass-art-oh)
You have	Ha (a)
You have spent / You spent / You did spend	Ha passato (a pass-art-oh)
We have	Abbiamo (ab-ee-arm-oh)
We have spent / We spent / We did spend	Abbiamo passato (ab-ee-arm-oh pass-art-oh)
September	settembre (se-tem-bray)
Christmas	il Natale (eel nat-arl-ay)
in Rome	a Roma (a roam-er)
in Italy	in Italia (een eet-al-yer)
in Switzerland	in Svizzera (een zvee-tser-er)
We have spent Christmas in Switzerland / We spent Christmas in Switzerland / We did spend Christmas in Switzerland.	Abbiamo passato il Natale in Svizzera. (ab-ee-arm-oh pass-art-oh eel nat-arl-ay een zvee-tser-er)
You have spent September in Italy / You spent September in Italy / You did spend September in Italy.	Ha passato settembre in Italia. (a pass-art-oh se-tem-bray een eet-al-yer)
and	e (ay)
It was	Era (air-ah)
It was fantastic.	Era fantastico. (air-ah fan-tass-teek-oh)
The weather was fantastic.	Il tempo era fantastico. (eel-tem-poe air-ah fan-tass-teek-oh)
I spent the weekend in Rome – and wow, the weather was fantastic.	Ho passato il weekend a Roma – e wow, il tempo era fantastico. (o pass-art-oh eel weekend a roam-er ay wow, eel-tem-poe air-ah fan-tass-teek-oh)

preparation	**preparazione** (prep-are-atz-ee-oh-nay)
prepared	**preparato** (pray-par-ay)
reservation	**prenotazione** (pray-no-tatz-ee-oh-nay)
reserved / booked	**prenotato** (pray-no-tart-oh)
ordered	**ordinato** (or-din-art-oh)
paid	**pagato** (pag-art-oh)
done	**fatto** (fat-oh)
the bill	**il conto** (eel kon-toe)
the dinner	**la cena** (la chain-er)
the coffee	**il caffè** (eel ka-fe)
a table	**un tavolo** (oon tav-oh-loe)
a room	**una camera** (oon-a cam-air-a)
a taxi	**un taxi** (oon taxi)
I have prepared the dinner / I prepared the dinner / I did prepare the dinner.	**Ho preparato la cena.** (o prep-are-art-oh la chain-er)
I have ordered coffee for dinner / I ordered coffee for dinner / I did order coffee for dinner.	**Ho ordinato il caffè per la cena.** (o or-din-art-oh eel ka-fe pair la chain-er)
I have booked a table for you / I booked a table for you / I did book a table for you.	**Ho prenotato un tavolo per Lei.** (o pray-no-tart-oh oon tav-oh-loe pair lay)
She has	**Lei ha** (lay a)
She has booked / reserved a table for this evening – She booked / reserved a table for this evening – She did book / reserve a table for this evening.	**Lei ha prenotato un tavolo per questa sera.** (lay a pray-no-tart-oh oon tav-oh-loe pair kwest-er sair-er)
He has	**Lui ha** (loo-ee a)
He has booked / reserved a room for two people – He booked / reserved a room for two people – He did book / reserve a room for two people.	**Lui ha prenotato una camera per due persone.** (loo-ee a pray-no-tart-oh oon-a cam-air-a pair doo-ay pair-soan-ay)

We have booked a taxi for you / We booked a taxi for you / We did book a taxi for you.	Abbiamo prenotato un taxi per Lei. (ab-ee-arm-oh pray-no-tart-oh oon taxi pair lay)
We paid the bill / We have paid the bill / We did pay the bill.	Abbiamo pagato il conto. (ab-ee-arm-oh pag-art-oh eel kon-toe)
What? / What thing?	Che cosa? (ke koe-ser)
What have you prepared? / What did you prepare? (literally "What thing you have prepared?")	Che cosa ha preparato? (ke koe-ser a prep-are-art-oh)
What have you done? / What did you do? (literally "What thing you have done?")	Che cosa ha fatto? (ke koe-ser a fat-oh)
I booked a table, ordered dinner and then paid the bill. What did you do?	Ho prenotato un tavolo, ordinato la cena e poi pagato il conto. Che cosa ha fatto? (o pray-no-tart-oh oon tav-oh-loe, or-din-art-oh la chain-er ey poy pag-art-oh eel kon-toe. ke koe-ser a fat-oh)
I'm planning to…	Ho intenzione di… (o in-ten-tzee-oh-nay dee)
I'm planning to go back to Italy in May.	Ho intenzione di ritornare in Italia a maggio. (o in-ten-tzee-oh-nay dee ri-torn-are-ay een eet-al-yer a madge-oh)
I'm scared of…	Ho paura di… (o pow-oo-rer dee)
I'm scared of going back to Italy in September.	Ho paura di ritornare in Italia a settembre. (o pow-oo-rer dee ri-torn-are-ay een eet-al-yer a se-tem-bray)
Really?	Veramente? (ve-ra-men-tay)
so (therefore)	quindi (kwin-dee)
but	ma (mu)
I feel like… / I fancy… (literally "I have want of…")	Ho voglia di… (o vol-ya dee)

Yes, I feel like / fancy going back to Rome but I'm scared of flying, so I'm planning to take the Eurostar.	Sì, ho voglia di ritornare a Roma ma ho paura di volare, quindi ho intenzione di prendere l'Eurostar. (see, o vol-ya dee ri-torn-are-ay a roam-er mu o pow-oo-rer dee vol-are-ay, kwin-dee o in-ten-tzee-oh-nay dee pren-de-rey lay-oo-roe-star)
I feel like / fancy buying something this morning.	Ho voglia di comprare qualcosa questa mattina. (o vol-ya dee com-prar-ay kwal-koe-zer kwest-er mat-een-er
He feels like / fancies reading something this afternoon.	Lui ha voglia di leggere qualcosa questo pomeriggio. (loo-ee a vol-ya dee ledge-er-ay kwal-koe-zer kwest-oh pom-air-idge-oh)
They have	Loro hanno (lo-roe an-oh)
They feel like eating something this evening.	Loro hanno voglia di mangiare qualcosa questa sera. (lo-roe an-oh vol-ya dee mange-are-ay kwal-koe-zer kwest-er sair-er)
I need... (literally "I have need of...")	Ho bisogno di... (o beez-on-yoe dee)
I need to speak Italian.	Ho bisogno di parlare italiano. (o beez-on-yoe dee par-lar-ay eet-al-ee-arn-oh)
I need a taxi.	Ho bisogno di un taxi. (o beez-on-yoe dee oon taxi)
I need a room.	Ho bisogno di una camera. (o beez-on-yoe dee oon-a cam-air-a)
I need help.	Ho bisogno di aiuto. (o bisogno di eye-oot-oh)
You need help, mate!	Hai bisogno di aiuto, amico! (eye bisogno di eye-oot-oh am-ee-koe)
I can't stand... / I hate... (literally "I have the horror of...")	Ho l'orrore di... (o lo-roar-ay dee)
I can't stand flying! / I hate flying!	Ho l'orrore di volare! (o lo-roar-ay dee vol-are-ay)

I can't stand living with my in-laws / I hate living with my in-laws.	Ho l'orrore di abitare con i miei suoceri. (o lo-roar-ay dee ab-it-are-ay kon ee mee-ay soo-o-chair-ee)
We can't stand eating with my parents / We hate eating with my parents.	Abbiamo l'orrore di mangiare con i miei genitori. (ab-ee-arm-oh lo-roar-ay dee mange-are-ay kon ee mee-ay jen-ee-tore-ee)
She can't stand working here / She hates working here.	Lei ha l'orrore di lavorare qui. (lay a lo-roar-ay dee lavo-or-are-ay kwee)
I was	Ero (air-oh)
solitary	solitario (sol-eet-are-ee-oh)
contrary	contrario (kon-trar-ee-oh)
ordinary	ordinario (or-deen-are-ee-oh)
I was ordinary.	Ero ordinario. (air-oh or-deen-are-ee-oh)
I was about to… / I was just about to… (literally "I stayed for…")	Stavo per… (starve-oh pair)
I was about to prepare the dinner / I was just about to prepare the dinner.	Stavo per preparare la cena. (starve-oh pair pray-par-are-ay la chain-er)
I was about to pay the bill.	Stavo per pagare il conto. (starve-oh pair pag-are-ay eel kon-toe)
I was just about to book a table.	Stavo per prenotare un tavolo. (starve-oh pair pray-note-are-ay oon tav-oh-loe)
You called me / You did call me / You have called me. (formal)	Mi ha chiamato. (mee a kee-am-art-oh)
You called me / You did call me / You have called me. (informal)	Mi hai chiamato. (mee eye kee-am-art-oh)
when	quando (kwan-doe)
I was just about to book a taxi when you called me. Really!	Stavo per prenotare un taxi quando mi hai chiamato. Veramente! (starve-oh pair pray-note-are-ay oon taxi kwan-doe mee eye kee-am-art-oh. ve-ra-men-tay)

I was about to leave when the telephone rang.	Stavo per partire quando il telefono ha squillato. (starve-oh pair part-ear-ray kwan-doe eel tel-off-on-oh a skwee-lar-toe
I was just about to phone you when you knocked at the door. (informal)	Stavo per telefonarti quando hai bussato alla porta. (starve-oh pair tel-ef-own-are-tee kwan-doe eye boos-art-oh al-la port-er)
I was just about to order a taxi when it started to rain.	Stavo per ordinare un taxi quando ha cominciato a piovere. (starve-oh pair or-din-are-ay oon taxi kwan-doe a kom-in-chart-oh a pee-oh-vair-ay)
so (extremely, very)	così (koh-see)
I was so romantic.	Ero così romantico. (air-oh koh-zee roe-man-teek-oh)
I was so illogical.	Ero così illogico. (air-oh koh-zee ee-lodge-eek-oh)
is	è (ay)
Mario is romantic.	Mario è romantico. (ma-ree-oh ay roe-man-teek-oh)
Maria is romantic.	Maria è romantica. (ma-ree-ah ay roe-man-teek-a)
I am	Sono (son-oh)
arrived	arrivato / arrivata (a-reev-art-oh / a-reev-art-a)
I have arrived / I arrived / I did arrive. (said by a man / boy)	Sono arrivato. (son-oh a-reev-art-oh)
I have arrived / I arrived / I did arrive. (said by a woman / girl)	Sono arrivata. (son-oh a-reev-art-a)
gone	andato / andata (and-art-oh / and-art-a)
I have gone / I went / I did go. (said by a man / boy)	Sono andato. (son-oh and-art-oh)
I have gone / I went / I did go. (said by a woman / girl)	Sono andata. (son-oh and-art-a)
You are (formal)	È (ay)

You have gone / You went / You did go. (said to a man / boy) – (formal)	È andato. (ay and-art-oh)
You have gone / You went / You did go. (said to a woman / girl) – (formal)	È andata. (ay and-art-a)
You have arrived / You arrived / You did arrive. (said to a man / boy) – (formal)	È arrivato. (ay a-reev-art-oh)
You have arrived / You arrived / You did arrive. (said to a woman / girl) – (formal)	È arrivata. (ay a-reev-art-a)
You are (informal)	Sei (say)
You have arrived / You arrived / You did arrive. (said to a man / boy) – (informal)	Sei arrivato. (say a-reev-art-oh)
You have arrived / You arrived / You did arrive. (said to a woman / girl) – (informal)	Sei arrivata. (say a-reev-art-a)
I'm sorry.	Mi dispiace. (mee dis-pee-arch-ey)
a little / a bit	un po' (oon po)
I was a little distracted.	Ero un po' distratto / distratta. (air-oh oon po dee-stra-toe / dee-stra-ta)
I'm sorry, I was in the middle of eating when you arrived. (informal)	Mi dispiace, stavo mangiando quando sei arrivato / arrivata. (mee dis-pee-arch-ey, starve-oh mange-and-oh kwan-doe say a-reev-art-oh / a-reev-art-a)
I'm sorry, I was in the middle of preparing dinner when you arrived, so I was a bit distracted. (informal)	Mi dispiace, stavo preparando la cena quando sei arrivato / arrivata, quindi ero un po' distratto / distratta. (mee dis-pee-arch-ey, starve-oh pray-par-ay la chain-er kwan-doe say a-reev-art-oh / a-reev-art-a kwin-dee air-oh oon po dee-stra-toe / dee-stra-ta)

I was in the middle of studying when my mother arrived.	**Stavo studiando quando mia madre è arrivata.** (starve-oh stood-ee-and-oh kwan-doe mee-a mard-re ay a-reev-art-a)
I was in the middle of cooking when you phoned me.	**Stavo cucinando quando mi hai telefonato.** (starve-oh koo-cheen-an-doe kwan-doe mee eye tay-lay-fone-art-oh)
I was in the middle of having dinner when your email arrived.	**Stavo cenando quando la tua e-mail è arrivata.** (starve-oh chen-an-deo kwan-doe la too-a ee-mail ay a-reev-art-a)

Wow, Chapter 6 all finished! With each chapter completed, the knowledge you have already gained becomes more secure and your horizons are gradually widened. Have a good break before the next one!

Learn the most common words first

Did you know that the 100 most common words in a language make up roughly 50% of everything you say in any given day, week, month or year? Or that the 500 most common words make up roughly 90% of everything you say?

Since these extremely common words are so useful, I recomment that, in addition to stealing words wherever you can, you should also focus as much as possible on those words that are used most often, as these will form the backbone of everything you say.

Of course, you may be wondering, how do I know which words are most common? Well, one way to find this out is to look at word frequency lists that you can find on the internet – boring!

Another method you can use, though, is to note down unfamiliar words whenever you see them. Don't bother looking them up right away though. Instead, put a tick next to them every time that you come across them.

Then, at the end of every month, take a look and see which words have the most ticks against them – these are the most common. Feel free now to look these up and write the translation next to all the ticks you've made.

Having written down the translation, don't try to remember it – instead, whenever you encounter those same words again, flick back to your notes and check the meaning.

Doing this each time will guarantee that your focus will always be on the most common words and that you will gradually begin to pick them up!

CHAPTER 7

I'm moving to Italy in July
because of you!
BECAUSE of me?
You mean *THANKS* to me!

I'm moving to Italy in July because of you!
BECAUSE of me? You mean *THANKS* to me!

You help someone change their life and this is the thanks you get!

Well, you probably already know how to be ungrateful in English, so let me teach you how to be ungrateful in Italian!

What is "this morning" in Italian?

questa mattina
(kwest-er mat-een-er)

And "this evening"?

questa sera
(kwest-er sair-er)

And "this afternoon"?

questo pomeriggio
(kwest-oh pom-air-idge-oh)

Notice how the word for "this" changes. Again, this is an example of the Mario-Maria Rule. Morning (mattina) and evening (sera) are both feminine in Italian, so the word for "this" which is used with them ends in an "a" – questa. Afternoon (pomeriggio) is masculine, so the word for "this" ends in a "o" – questo.

What is "September" in Italian?

settembre
(se-tem-bray)

The months of the year in Italian are all masculine, so, with this in mind, how would you say "this September"?

questo settembre
(kwest-oh se-tem-bray)

What is "May" in Italian?

maggio
(madge-oh)

So how would you say "this May"?

questo maggio
(kwest-oh madge-oh)

"July" in Italian is:

luglio
(lool-yoh)

So what would "this July" be?

questo luglio
(kwest-oh lool-yoh)

And again, how would you say "I visited"?

Ho visitato
(o visit-art-oh)

And what about "I visited Rome"?

Ho visitato Roma.
(o visit-art-oh roam-er)

So, how would you say "I visited Rome this July"?

Ho visitato Roma questo luglio.
(o visit-art-oh roam-er kwest-oh lool-yoh)

What is "I'm planning to..."?

Ho intenzione di...
(o in-ten-tzee-oh-nay dee)

"Visit" or "to visit" in Italian is:

visitare
(visit-are-ay)

Okay, how would you say "I'm planning to visit..."?

Ho intenzione di visitare...
(o in-ten-tzee-oh-nay dee visit-are-ay)

And how would you say "I'm planning to visit Rome this July"?

Ho intenzione di visitare Roma questo luglio.
(o in-ten-tzee-oh-nay dee visit-are-ay roam-er kwest-oh lool-yoh)

What is "to go back" or "to return" in Italian?

ritornare
(ree-torn-are-ay)

So, how would you say "I'm planning to go back"?

Ho intenzione di ritornare.
(o in-ten-tzee-oh-nay dee ree-torn-are-ay)

And what is "in Italy" or "to Italy"?

in Italia
(*een eet-al-yer*)

Alright, how would you say "I'm planning to go back to Italy this July"?

Ho intenzione di ritornare in Italia questo luglio.
(*o in-ten-tzee-oh-nay dee ri-torn-are-ay een eet-al-yer kwest-oh lool-yoh*)

"I'm moving" in Italian is:

Mi trasferisco
(*mee tras-fur-ees-koh*)

It's always useful when learning a foreign language to understand what each of the bits in the sentence actually mean.

"I'm moving" in Italian is a good example of this – of how knowing what each word actually means can make the words both more memorable and more understandable.

In this example, "trasferisco" means "I transfer" or "I'm transferring".

"Mi" means "myself". So, "I'm moving" in Italian is "I'm transferring myself" or, in absolutely literal terms, "myself I transfer".

It is well worth trying to see if you can break expressions into bits like this, because when you really understand what they mean literally, this often makes them far easier to remember.

So, again, "I'm moving" in Italian is literally "I'm transferring myself" or "myself I transfer", which is:

Mi trasferisco
(*mee tras-fur-ees-koh*)

Now, how would you say "to Italy"?

in Italia
(*een eet-al-yer*)

And again, what is "I'm moving" (literally "myself I transfer")?

Mi trasferisco
(*mee tras-fur-ees-koh*)

So, how would you say "I'm moving to Italy"?

Mi trasferisco in Italia.
(mee tras-fur-ees-koh een eet-al-yer)

How about "I'm moving to Italy this July?"

Mi trasferisco in Italia questo luglio.
(mee tras-fur-ees-koh een eet-al-yer kwest-oh lool-yoh)

What about "I'm moving to Italy this September"?

Mi trasferisco in Italia questo settembre.
(mee tras-fur-ees-koh een eet-al-yer kwest-oh se-tem-bray)

And how would you say "in Rome" or "to Rome"?

a Roma
(a roam-er)

How would you say "I'm moving to Rome this September"?

Mi trasferisco a Roma questo settembre.
(mee tras-fur-ees-koh a roam-er kwest-oh se-tem-bray)

"Because of you" (informal) in Italian, is:

per causa tua
(pair kow-zer too-er)

Literally, this means "for cause your". So, it's a bit like saying "it's your cause", "it's your fault", or "it's because of you".

Now again, how would you say "I'm moving to Rome this September"?

Mi trasferisco a Roma questo settembre.
(mee tras-fur-ees-koh a roam-er kwest-oh se-tem-bray)

Let's try saying "I'm moving to Rome this September because of you!" (informal) – (literally "Myself I transfer to Rome this September for cause your!"):

Mi trasferisco a Roma questo settembre per causa tua!
(mee tras-fur-ees-koh a roam-er kwest-oh se-tem-bray pair kow-zer too-er)

Now try "I'm moving to Rome this July because of you!" (informal):

Mi trasferisco a Roma questo luglio per causa tua!
(mee tras-fur-ees-koh a roam-er kwest-oh lool-yoh pair kow-zer too-er)

What is "to Italy"?

in Italia
(een eet-al-yer)

How would you say "I'm moving to Italy this July because of you!" (informal)?

Mi trasferisco in Italia questo luglio per causa tua!
(mee tras-fur-ees-koh een eet-al-yer kwest-oh lool-yoh pair kow-zer too-er)

And again, on its own, what is "because of you"?

per causa tua
(pair kow-zer too-er)

So, as I've said, this literally means "for cause your", to show it's "your" fault.

"Because of me" in Italian works in the same way – you will say literally "for cause my", which is:

per causa mia
(pair kow-zer mee-er)

Turn this into a question now by raising your voice at the end and ask "because of me?" (literally "for cause my?"):

Per causa mia?
(pair kow-zer mee-er)

So, you have now been introduced to how Italians express the idea "because of". It is a very useful expression, which can be used both in a fairly neutral way or, if you want, in a very negative way to attribute blame: "I lost my money because of you!" or "I never got married because of you!" Heady stuff, yes!

"Because of" actually has a partner that has a similar meaning except that it is more positive and means "thanks to…". You will want to use this phrase for nice things, such as "Thanks to you, I found my money in the end" or "Thanks to you, I met and married a wonderful person!".

"Thanks to..." in Italian is:

Grazie a...
(**grats-ee-ey** a)

"me" in Italian is:

me
(*mey*)

So how would you say "thanks to me!"?

Grazie a me!
(*grats-ee-ey a mey*)

And again, what was "because of me"?

per causa mia
(*pair kow-zer mee-er*)

So, literally, this is "for cause *my*".

And again, how would you say "thanks to me!"?

Grazie a me!
(*grats-ee-ey a mey*)

"Do you want...?" (informal) in Italian is:

Vuoi...?
(**vwoy**)

Literally, "vuoi" means "you want" but if you raise your voice as you say it, it becomes a question, literally "you want?" – "vuoi?".

So, how would you say "do you want to prepare the dinner?" (informal) – (literally "you want to prepare the dinner?")?

Vuoi preparare la cena?
(*vwoy pray-par-are-ay la chain-er*)

What is "this evening" in Italian?

questa sera
(*kwest-er sair-er*)

How would you say "do you want to prepare the dinner this evening?" (informal)?

Vuoi preparare la cena questa sera?
(vwoy pray-par-are-ay la chain-er kwest-er sair-er)

What is "to eat something"?

mangiare qualcosa
(mange-are-ay kwal-koe-zer)

How would you now say "do you want to eat something?" (informal)?

Vuoi mangiare qualcosa?
(vwoy mange-are-ay kwal-koe-zer)

How about "do you want to buy something?" (informal)?

Vuoi comprare qualcosa?
(vwoy com-prar-ay kwal-koe-zer)

What is "to pay the bill"?

pagare il conto
(pag-are-ay eel kon-toe)

So, how would you say "do you want to pay the bill?" (informal)?

Vuoi pagare il conto?
(vwoy pag-are-ay eel kon-toe)

How about "do you want to book a taxi?" (informal)?

Vuoi prenotare un taxi?
(vwoy pray-note-are-ay oon taxi)

"Do you want to go back to Italy this July?" (informal)?

Vuoi ritornare in Italia questo luglio?
(vwoy ri-torn-are-ay een eet-al-yer kwest-oh lool-yoh)

So "do you want...?" (informal) as a question is:

Vuoi...?
(vwoy)

"You want" (informal) as a statement is the same, except you don't raise your voice as you say it. So, "you want" will simply be:

Vuoi
(vwoy)

So, how would you say as a statement "you want to go back to Italy this July!" (informal)?

Vuoi ritornare in Italia questo luglio!
(vwoy ri-torn-are-ay een eet-al-yer kwest-oh lool-yoh)

And how about "you want to go back to Rome this July!" (informal)?

Vuoi ritornare a Roma questo luglio!
(vwoy ri-torn-are-ay a roam-er kwest-oh lool-yoh)

And how would you say "you want to pay the bill!" (informal)?

Vuoi pagare il conto!
(vwoy pag-are-ay eel kon-toe)

"To say" in Italian is:

dire
(dear-ay)

How would you say "you want to say" (informal)?

Vuoi dire
(vwoy dear-ay)

Interestingly, "you want to say" is actually the way that Italian speakers say "you mean". If for example, an Italian person wants to say "what do you mean?" then they will ask "what do you want to say?".

So, to begin with, how would you say "you mean" in Italian (informal) – (literally "you want to say")?

Vuoi dire
(vwoy dear-ay)

And again, what is "thanks to..."?

grazie a...
(grats-ee-ey)

And "thanks to me"?

grazie a me
(grats-ee-ey a mey)

And once more, how would you say "you mean" (informal) – (literally "you want to say")?

Vuoi dire
(vwoy dear-ay)

How would you say "you mean *thanks* to me!" (informal)?

Vuoi dire *grazie* a me!
(vwoy dear-ay grats-ee-ey a mey)

Right, let's go back to our initial dialogue. To begin with, how would someone say "I'm moving to Italy" (literally "Myself I transfer to Italy")?

Mi trasferisco in Italia.
(mee tras-fur-ees-koh een eet-al-yer)

And how would you say "this July"?

questo luglio
(kwest-oh lool-yoh)

And again, how would you say "because of you" (informal) – (literally "for cause your")?

per causa tua
(pair kow-zer too-er)

Putting this together, how would you say "I'm moving to Italy this July because of you!" (informal)?

Mi trasferisco in Italia questo luglio per causa tua!
(mee tras-fur-ees-koh een eet-al-yer kwest-oh lool-yoh pair kow-zer too-er)

And what is "because of me"?

per causa mia
(pair kow-zer mee-er)

How would you reply "Because of me? You mean *thanks* to me!" (informal) –
(literally "For cause my? You want to say thanks to me!")?

Per causa mia? Vuoi dire *grazie* a me!
(pair kow-zer mee-er vwoy dear-ay grats-ee-ey a mey)

Now try the entire dialogue below and see how you get on. Take your time and think out each step bit by bit until it all comes naturally and effortlessly. And remember, there's no rush!

I'm moving to Italy this July because of you! (informal)
Mi trasferisco in Italia questo luglio per causa tua!
(mee tras-fur-ees-koh een eet-al-yer kwest-oh lool-yoh pair kow-zer too-er)

Because of me? You mean *thanks* to me! (informal)
Per causa mia? Vuoi dire *grazie* a me!
(pair kow-zer mee-er vwoy dear-ay grats-ee-ey a mey)

Building Blocks 7

Some especially useful building blocks this time, I'm sure you'll agree:

vado
(var-doe)
go/am going

in realtà
(een ray-al-ta)
actually/
in fact*1

anch'io
(arnk-ee-oh)
I too/
I also*2

il mese prossimo
(eel may-zay
pross-ee-moe)
next month*3

a Firenze
(a fee-rents-ey)
to Florence

l'anno prossimo
(lan-oh
pross-ee-moe)
next year*4

*1 literally "in reality"

*2 literally "also I"

*3 literally "the month approaching"

*4 literally "the year approaching"

There are five columns on this occasion. More columns of course equal even more fun!

in realtà
(een ray-al-ta)
actually/
in fact*1

anch'io
(arnk-ee-oh)
I too/
I also*2

mi trasferisco
(mee tras-fur-ees-koh)
move/
am moving*3

a Firenze
(a fee-rents-ey)
to Florence

il mese prossimo
(eel may-zay pross-ee-moe)
next month*4

vado
(var-doe)
go/am going

a Roma
(a roam-er)
to Rome

in Italia
(een eet-al-yer)
to Italy

l'anno prossimo
(lan-oh pross-ee-moe)
next year*5

*1 literally "in reality"

*2 literally "also I"

*3 literally "Myself I transfer"

*4 literally "the month approaching"

*5 literally "the year approaching"

Checklist 7

The penultimate checklist – you're almost there...

il weekend (eel weekend)	the weekend
romantico (roe-man-teek-oh)	romantic
fantastico (fan-tass-teek-oh)	fantastic
politico (pol-ee-teek-oh)	political
illogico (ee-lodge-eek-oh)	illogical
entusiasta (en-tooze-ee-ast-a)	enthusiastic
Ho (o)	I have
visitato (visit-art-oh)	visited
Ho visitato (o visit-art-oh)	I have visited / I visited / I did visit
Roma (roam-er)	Rome
Napoli (nap-oh-lee)	Naples

Ho visitato Napoli. (o visit-art-oh nap-oh-lee)	I have visited Naples / I visited Naples / I did visit Naples.
passato (pass-art-oh)	spent
Ho passato (o pass-art-oh)	I have spent / I spent / I did spend
Ha (a)	You have
Ha passato (a pass-art-oh)	You have spent / You spent / You did spend
Abbiamo (ab-ee-arm-oh)	We have
Abbiamo passato (ab-ee-arm-oh pass-art-oh)	We have spent / We spent / We did spend
settembre (se-tem-bray)	September
il Natale (eel nat-arl-ay)	Christmas
a Roma (a roam-er)	in Rome
in Italia (een eet-al-yer)	in Italy
in Svizzera (een zvee-tser-er)	in Switzerland
Abbiamo passato il Natale in Svizzera. (ab-ee-arm-oh pass-art-oh eel nat-arl-ay een zvee-tser-er)	We have spent Christmas in Switzerland / We spent Christmas in Switzerland / We did spend Christmas in Switzerland.
Ha passato settembre in Italia. (a pass-art-oh se-tem-bray een eet-al-yer)	You have spent September in Italy / You spent September in Italy / You did spend September in Italy.
e (ay)	and
Era (air-ah)	It was
Era fantastico. (air-ah fan-tass-teek-oh)	It was fantastic.
Il tempo era fantastico. (eel-tem-poe air-ah fan-tass-teek-oh)	The weather was fantastic.
Ho passato il weekend a Roma – e wow, il tempo era fantastico. (o pass-art-oh eel weekend a roam-er ay wow, eel-tem-poe air-ah fan-tass-teek-oh)	I spent the weekend in Rome – and wow, the weather was fantastic.
preparazione (prep-are-atz-ee-oh-nay)	preparation
preparato (pray-par-ato)	prepared

prenotazione (pray-no-tatz-ee-oh-nay)	reservation
prenotato (pray-no-tart-oh)	reserved / booked
ordinato (or-din-art-oh)	ordered
pagato (pag-art-oh)	paid
fatto (fat-oh)	done
il conto (eel kon-toe)	the bill
la cena (la chain-er)	the dinner
il caffè (eel ka-fe)	the coffee
un tavolo (oon tav-oh-loe)	a table
una camera (oon-a cam-air-a)	a room
un taxi (oon taxi)	a taxi
Ho preparato la cena. (o prep-are-art-oh la chain-er)	I have prepared the dinner / I prepared the dinner / I did prepare the dinner.
Ho ordinato il caffè per la cena. (o or-din-art-oh eel ka-fe pair la chain-er)	I have ordered coffee for dinner / I ordered coffee for dinner / I did order coffee for dinner.
Ho prenotato un tavolo per Lei. (o pray-no-tart-oh oon tav-oh-loe pair lay)	I have booked a table for you / I booked a table for you / I did book a table for you.
Lei ha (lay a)	She has
Lei ha prenotato un tavolo per questa sera. (lay a pray-no-tart-oh oon tav-oh-loe pair kwest-er sair-er)	She has booked / reserved a table for this evening – She booked / reserved a table for this evening – She did book / reserve a table for this evening.
Lui ha (loo-ee a)	He has
Lui ha prenotato una camera per due persone. (loo-ee a pray-no-tart-oh oon-a cam-air-a pair doo-ay pair-soan-ay)	He has booked / reserved a room for two people – He booked / reserved a room for two people – He did book / reserve a room for two people.
Abbiamo prenotato un taxi per Lei. (ab-ee-arm-oh pray-no-tart-oh oon taxi pair lay)	We have booked a taxi for you / We booked a taxi for you / We did book a taxi for you.
Abbiamo pagato il conto. (ab-ee-arm-oh pag-art-oh eel kon-toe)	We paid the bill / We have paid the bill / We did pay the bill.

Che cosa? (ke koe-ser)	What? / What thing?
Che cosa ha preparato? (ke koe-ser a prep-are-art-oh)	What have you prepared? / What did you prepare? (literally "What thing you have prepared?")
Che cosa ha fatto? (ke koe-ser a fat-oh)	What have you done? / What did you do? (literally "What thing you have done?")
Ho prenotato un tavolo, ordinato la cena e poi pagato il conto. Che cosa ha fatto? (o pray-no-tart-oh oon tav-oh-loe, or-din-art-oh la chain-er ey poy pag-art-oh eel kon-toe. ke koe-ser a fat-oh)	I booked a table, ordered dinner and then paid the bill. What did you do?
Ho intenzione di... (o in-ten-tzee-oh-nay dee)	I'm planning to... (literally "I have intention of...")
Ho intenzione di ritornare in Italia a maggio. (o in-ten-tzee-oh-nay dee ri-torn-are-ay een eet-al-yer a madge-oh)	I'm planning to go back to Italy in May.
Ho paura di... (o pow-oo-rer dee)	I'm scared of... (literally "I have fear of...")
Ho paura di ritornare in Italia a settembre. (o pow-oo-rer dee ri-torn-are-ay een eet-al-yer a se-tem-bray)	I'm scared of going back to Italy in September.
Veramente? (ve-ra-men-tay)	Really?
quindi (kwin-dee)	so (therefore)
ma (mu)	but
Ho voglia di... (o vol-ya dee)	I feel like... / I fancy... (literally "I have want of...")
Sì, ho voglia di ritornare a Roma ma ho paura di volare, quindi ho intenzione di prendere l'Eurostar. (see, o vol-ya dee ri-torn-are-ay a roam-er mu o pow-oo-rer dee vol-are-ay, kwin-dee o in-ten-tzee-oh-nay dee pren-de-rey lay-oo-roe-star)	Yes, I feel like going back to Rome but I'm scared of flying, so I'm planning to take the Eurostar.

Ho voglia di comprare qualcosa questa mattina. (o vol-ya dee com-prar-ay kwal-koe-zer kwest-er mat-een-er	I feel like / fancy buying something this morning.
Lui ha voglia di leggere qualcosa questo pomeriggio. (loo-ee a vol-ya dee ledge-er-ay kwal-koe-zer kwest-oh pom-air-idge-oh)	He feels like / fancies reading something this afternoon.
Loro hanno (lo-roe an-oh)	They have
Loro hanno voglia di mangiare qualcosa questa sera. (lo-roe an-oh vol-ya dee mange-are-ay kwal-koe-zer kwest-er sair-er)	They feel like / fancy eating something this evening.
Ho bisogno di... (o beez-on-yoe dee)	I need... (literally "I have need of...")
Ho bisogno di parlare italiano. (o beez-on-yoe dee par-lar-ay eet-al-ee-arn-oh)	I need to speak Italian.
Ho bisogno di un taxi. (o beez-on-yoe dee oon taxi)	I need a taxi.
Ho bisogno di una camera. (o beez-on-yoe dee oon-a cam-air-a)	I need a room.
Ho bisogno di aiuto. (o bisogno di eye-oot-oh)	I need help.
Hai bisogno di aiuto, amico! (eye bisogno di eye-oot-oh am-ee-koe)	You need help, mate!
Ho l'orrore di... (o lo-roar-ay dee)	I can't stand... / I hate... (literally "I have the horror of...")
Ho l'orrore di volare! (o lo-roar-ay dee vol-are-ay)	I can't stand flying! / I hate flying!
Ho l'orrore di abitare con i miei suoceri. (o lo-roar-ay dee ab-it-are-ay kon ee mee-ay soo-o-chair-ee)	I can't stand living with my in-laws / I hate living with my in-laws.
Abbiamo l'orrore di mangiare con i miei genitori. (ab-ee-arm-oh lo-roar-ay dee mange-are-ay kon ee mee-ay jen-ee-tore-ee)	We can't stand eating with my parents / We hate eating with my parents.

Lei ha l'orrore di lavorare qui. (lay a lo-roar-ay dee lavo-or-are-ay kwee)	She can't stand working here / She hates working here.
Ero (air-oh)	I was
solitario (sol-eet-are-ee-oh)	solitary
contrario (kon-trar-ee-oh)	contrary
ordinario (or-deen-are-ee-oh)	ordinary
Ero ordinario. (air-oh or-deen-are-ee-oh)	I was ordinary.
Stavo per... (starve-oh pair)	I was about to... / I was just about to... (literally "I stayed for...")
Stavo per preparare la cena. (starve-oh pair pray-par-are-ay la chain-er)	I was about to prepare the dinner / I was just about to prepare the dinner.
Stavo per pagare il conto. (starve-oh pair pag-are-ay eel kon-toe)	I was about to pay the bill.
Stavo per prenotare un tavolo. (starve-oh pair pray-note-are-ay oon tav-oh-loe)	I was just about to book a table.
Mi ha chiamato. (mee a kee-am-art-oh)	You called me / You did call me / You have called me. (formal)
Mi hai chiamato. (mee eye kee-am-art-oh)	You called me / You did call me / You have called me. (informal)
quando (kwan-doe)	when
Stavo per prenotare un taxi quando mi hai chiamato. Veramente! (starvo-oh pair pray-note-are-ay oon taxi kwan-doe mee eye kee-am-art-oh. ve-ra-men-tay)	I was just about to book a taxi when you called me. Really!
Stavo per partire quando il telefono ha squillato. (starve-oh pair part-ear-ray kwan-doe eel tel-off-on-oh a skwee-lar-toe	I was about to leave when the telephone rang.
Stavo per telefonarti quando hai bussato alla porta. (starve-oh pair tel-ef-own-are-tee kwan-doe eye boos-art-oh al-la port-er)	I was just about to phone you when you knocked at the door. (informal)

Stavo per ordinare un taxi quando ha cominciato a piovere. (starve-oh pair or-din-are-ay oon taxi kwan-doe a kom-in-chart-oh a pee-oh-vair-ay)	I was just about to order a taxi when it started to rain.
così (koh-see)	so (extremely, very)
Ero così romantico. (air-oh koh-zee roe-man-teek-oh)	I was so romantic.
Ero così illogico. (air-oh koh-zee ee-lodge-eek-oh)	I was so illogical.
è (ay)	is
Mario è romantico. (ma-ree-oh ay roe-man-teek-oh)	Mario is romantic.
Maria è romantica. (ma-ree-ah ay roe-man-teek-a)	Maria is romantic.
Sono (son-oh)	I am
arrivato / arrivata (a-reev-art-oh / a-reev-art-a)	arrived
Sono arrivato. (son-oh a-reev-art-oh)	I have arrived / I arrived / I did arrive. (said by a man / boy)
Sono arrivata. (son-oh a-reev-art-a)	I have arrived / I arrived / I did arrive. (said by a woman / girl)
andato / andata (and-art-oh / and-art-a)	gone
Sono andato. (son-oh and-art-oh)	I have gone / I went / I did go. (said by a man / boy)
Sono andata. (son-oh and-art-oh)	I have gone / I went / I did go. (said by a woman / girl)
È (ay)	You are (formal)
È andato. (ay and-art-oh)	You have gone / You went / You did go. (said to a man / boy) – (formal)
È andata. (ay and-art-oh)	You have gone / You went / You did go. (said to a woman / girl) – (formal)
È arrivato. (ay a-reev-art-oh)	You have arrived / You arrived / You did arrive. (said to a man / boy) – (formal)

È arrivata. (ay a-reev-art-a)	You have arrived / You arrived / You did arrive. (said to a woman / girl) – (formal)
Sei (say)	You are (informal)
Sei arrivato. (say a-reev-art-oh)	You have arrived / You arrived / You did arrive. (said to a man / boy) – (informal)
Sei arrivata. (say a-reev-art-a)	You have arrived / You arrived / You did arrive. (said to a woman / girl) – (informal)
Mi dispiace. (mee dis-pee-arch-ey)	I'm sorry.
un po' (oon po)	a little / a bit
Ero un po' distratto / distratta. (air-oh oon po dee-stra-toe / dee-stra-ta)	I was a little distracted.
Mi dispiace, stavo mangiando quando sei arrivato / arrivata. (mee dis-pee-arch-ey, starve-oh mange-and-oh kwan-doe say a-reev-art-oh / a-reev-art-a)	I'm sorry, I was in the middle of eating when you arrived. (informal)
Mi dispiace, stavo preparando la cena quando sei arrivato / arrivata, quindi ero un po' distratto / distratta. (mee dis-pee-arch-ey, starve-oh pray-par-ay la chain-er kwan-doe say a-reev-art-oh / a-reev-art-a kwin-dee air-oh oon po dee-stra-toe / dee-stra-ta)	I'm sorry, I was in the middle of preparing dinner when you arrived, so I was a bit distracted. (informal)
Stavo studiando quando mia madre è arrivata. (starve-oh stood-ee-and-oh kwan-doe mee-a mard-re ay a-reev-art-a)	I was in the middle of studying when my mother arrived.
Stavo cucinando quando mi hai telefonato. (starve-oh koo-cheen-an-doe kwan-doe mee eye tay-lay-fone-art-oh)	I was in the middle of cooking when you phoned me.

Stavo cenando quando la tua e-mail è arrivata. (starve-oh chen-an-deo kwan-doe la too-a ee-mail ay a-reev-art-a)	I was in the middle of having dinner when your email arrived.
luglio (lool-yoh)	July
questo luglio (kwest-oh lool-yoh)	this July
Ho visitato Roma questo luglio. (o visit-art-oh roam-er kwest-oh lool-yoh)	I visited Rome this July / I have visited Rome this July / I did visit Rome this July.
Ho intenzione di visitare Roma questo luglio. (o in-ten-tzee-oh-nay dee visit-are-ay roam-er kwest-oh lool-yoh)	I'm planning to visit Rome this July.
Mi trasferisco (mee tras-fur-ees-koh)	I'm moving (literally "Myself I transfer")
Mi trasferisco in Italia questo settembre. (mee tras-fur-ees-koh een eet-al-yer kwest-oh se-tem-bray)	I'm moving to Italy this September.
per causa tua (pair kow-zer too-er)	because of you (informal)
grazie a... (grats-ee-ey)	thanks to...
Grazie a me! (grats-ee-ey a mey)	Thanks to me!
Mi trasferisco in Italia questo luglio per causa tua! (mee tras-fur-ees-koh een eet-al-yer kwest-oh lool-yoh a roam-er pair kow-zer too-er)	I'm moving to Italy this July because of you! (informal)
Vuoi? (vwoy)	Do you want? (literally "Want you?") – (informal)
Vuoi preparare la cena questa sera? (vwoy pray-par-are-ay la chain-er kwest-er sair-er)	Do you want to prepare the dinner this evening? (informal)
Vuoi mangiare qualcosa? (vwoy mange-are-ay kwal-koe-zer)	Do you want to eat something? (informal)
Vuoi (vwoy)	You want (informal)
dire (dear-ay)	to say
Vuoi dire (vwoy dear-ay)	You mean (literally "You want to say") – (informal)

Mi trasferisco in Italia questo luglio per causa tua! (mee tras-fur-ees-koh een eet-al-yer kwest-oh lool-yoh a roam-er pair kow-zer too-er)	I'm moving to Italy this July because of you! (informal)
Per causa **mia? Vuoi dire** *"grazie a* **me"!** (pair kow-zer mee-er vwoy dear-ay grats-ee-ey a mey)	*Because* of me? You mean *thanks* to me! (informal)
in realtà (een ray-al-ta)	actually / in fact
anch'io (arnk-ee-o)	I too / I also
In realtà, anch'io mi trasferisco a Firenze. (een ray-al-ta, arnk-ee-o mee tras-fur-ees-koh a fee-rents-ey)	Actually, I'm moving to Florence too.
In realtà, anch'io mi trasferisco in Italia il mese prossimo. (een ray-al-ta, arnk-ee-o mee tras-fur-ees-koh een eet-al-yer eel may-zay pross-ee-moe)	Actually, I'm also moving to Italy next month.
In realtà, anch'io vado a Roma l'anno prossimo. (een ray-al-ta, arnk-ee-o var-doe a roam-er lan-oh pross-ee-moe)	Actually, I'm also going to Rome next year.

Flip-flop time!

the weekend	**il weekend** (eel weekend)
romantic	**romantico** (roe-man-teek-oh)
fantastic	**fantastico** (fan-tass-teek-oh)
political	**politico** (pol-ee-teek-oh)
illogical	**illogico** (ee-lodge-eek-oh)
enthusiastic	**entusiasta** (en-tooze-ee-ast-a)
I have	**Ho** (o)
visited	**visitato** (visit-art-oh)
I have visited / I visited / I did visit	**Ho visitato** (o visit-art-oh)
Rome	**Roma** (roam-er)

Naples	Napoli (nap-oh-lee)
I have visited Naples / I visited Naples / I did visit Naples.	Ho visitato Napoli. (o visit-art-oh nap-oh-lee)
spent	passato (pass-art-oh)
I have spent / I spent / I did spend	Ho passato (o pass-art-oh)
You have	Ha (a)
You have spent / You spent / You did spend	Ha passato (a pass-art-oh)
We have	Abbiamo (ab-ee-arm-oh)
We have spent / We spent / We did spend	Abbiamo passato (ab-ee-arm-oh pass-art-oh)
September	settembre (se-tem-bray)
Christmas	il Natale (eel nat-arl-ay)
in Rome	a Roma (a roam-er)
in Italy	in Italia (een eet-al-yer)
in Switzerland	in Svizzera (een zvee-tser-er)
We have spent Christmas in Switzerland / We spent Christmas in Switzerland / We did spend Christmas in Switzerland.	Abbiamo passato il Natale in Svizzera. (ab-ee-arm-oh pass-art-oh eel nat-arl-ay een zvee-tser-er)
You have spent September in Italy / You spent September in Italy / You did spend September in Italy.	Ha passato settembre in Italia. (a pass-art-oh se-tem-bray een eet-al-yer)
and	e (ay)
It was	Era (air-ah)
It was fantastic.	Era fantastico. (air-ah fan-tass-teek-oh)
The weather was fantastic.	Il tempo era fantastico. (eel-tem-poe air-ah an-tass-teek-oh)
I spent the weekend in Rome – and wow, the weather was fantastic.	Ho passato il weekend a Roma – e wow, il tempo era fantastico. (o pass-art-oh eel weekend a roam-er ay wow, eel-tem-poe air-ah fan-tass-teek-oh)

preparation	preparazione (prep-are-atz-ee-oh-nay)
prepared	preparato (pray-par-ay)
reservation	prenotazione (pray-no-tatz-ee-oh-nay)
reserved / booked	prenotato (pray-no-tart-oh)
ordered	ordinato (or-din-art-oh)
paid	pagato (pag-art-oh)
done	fatto (fat-oh)
the bill	il conto (eel kon-toe)
the dinner	la cena (la chain-er)
the coffee	il caffè (eel ka-fe)
a table	un tavolo (oon tav-oh-loe)
a room	una camera (oon-a cam-air-a)
a taxi	un taxi (oon taxi)
I have prepared the dinner / I prepared the dinner / I did prepare the dinner.	Ho preparato la cena. (o prep-are-art-oh la chain-er)
I have ordered coffee for dinner / I ordered coffee for dinner / I did order coffee for dinner.	Ho ordinato il caffè per la cena. (o or-din-art-oh eel ka-fe pair la chain-er)
I have booked a table for you / I booked a table for you / I did book a table for you.	Ho prenotato un tavolo per Lei. (o pray-no-tart-oh oon tav-oh-loe pair lay)
She has	Lei ha (lay a)
She has booked / reserved a table for this evening – She booked / reserved a table for this evening – She did book / reserve a table for this evening.	Lei ha prenotato un tavolo per questa sera. (lay a pray-no-tart-oh oon tav-oh-loe pair kwest-er sair-er)
He has	Lui ha (loo-ee a)
He has booked / reserved a room for two people – He booked / reserved a room for two people – He did book / reserve a room for two people.	Lui ha prenotato una camera per due persone. (loo-ee a pray-no-tart-oh oon-a cam-air-a pair doo-ay pair-soan-ay)

We have booked a taxi for you / We booked a taxi for you / We did book a taxi for you.	Abbiamo prenotato un taxi per Lei. (ab-ee-arm-oh pray-no-tart-oh oon taxi pair lay)
We paid the bill / We have paid the bill / We did pay the bill.	Abbiamo pagato il conto. (ab-ee-arm-oh pag-art-oh eel kon-toe)
What? / What thing?	Che cosa? (ke koe-ser)
What have you prepared? / What did you prepare? (literally "What thing you have prepared?")	Che cosa ha preparato? (ke koe-ser a prep-are-art-oh)
What have you done? / What did you do? (literally "What thing you have done?")	Che cosa ha fatto? (ke koe-ser a fat-oh)
I booked a table, ordered dinner and then paid the bill. What did you do?	Ho prenotato un tavolo, ordinato la cena e poi pagato il conto. Che cosa ha fatto? (o pray-no-tart-oh oon tav-oh-loe, or-din-art-oh la chain-er ey poy pag-art-oh eel kon-toe. ke koe-ser a fat-oh)
I'm planning to…	Ho intenzione di… (o in-ten-tzee-oh-nay dee)
I'm planning to go back to Italy in May.	Ho intenzione di ritornare in Italia a maggio. (o in-ten-tzee-oh-nay dee ri-torn-are-ay een eet-al-yer a madge-oh)
I'm scared of…	Ho paura di… (o pow-oo-rer dee)
I'm scared of going back to Italy in September.	Ho paura di ritornare in Italia a settembre. (o pow-oo-rer dee ri-torn-are-ay een eet-al-yer a se-tem-bray)
Really?	Veramente? (ve-ra-men-tay)
so (therefore)	quindi (kwin-dee)
but	ma (mu)
I feel like… / I fancy… (literally "I have want of…")	Ho voglia di… (o vol-ya dee)

Yes, I feel like / fancy going back to Rome but I'm scared of flying, so I'm planning to take the Eurostar.	Sì, ho voglia di ritornare a Roma ma ho paura di volare, quindi ho intenzione di prendere l'Eurostar. (see, o vol-ya dee ri-torn-are-ay a roam-er mu o pow-oo-rer dee vol-are-ay, kwin-dee o in-ten-tzee-oh-nay dee pren-de-rey lay-oo-roe-star)
I feel like / fancy buying something this morning.	Ho voglia di comprare qualcosa questa mattina. (o vol-ya dee com-prar-ay kwal-koe-zer kwest-er mat-een-er
He feels like / fancies reading something this afternoon.	Lui ha voglia di leggere qualcosa questo pomeriggio. (loo-ee a vol-ya dee ledge-er-ay kwal-koe-zer kwest-oh pom-air-idge-oh)
They have	Loro hanno (lo-roe an-oh)
They feel like eating something this evening.	Loro hanno voglia di mangiare qualcosa questa sera. (lo-roe an-oh vol-ya dee mange-are-ay kwal-koe-zer kwest-er sair-er)
I need... (literally "I have need of...")	Ho bisogno di... (o beez-on-yoe dee)
I need to speak Italian.	Ho bisogno di parlare italiano. (o beez-on-yoe dee par-lar-ay eet-al-ee-arn-oh)
I need a taxi.	Ho bisogno di un taxi. (o beez-on-yoe dee oon taxi)
I need a room.	Ho bisogno di una camera. (o beez-on-yoe dee oon-a cam-air-a)
I need help.	Ho bisogno di aiuto. (o bisogno di eye-oot-oh)
You need help, mate!	Hai bisogno di aiuto, amico! (eye bisogno di eye-oot-oh am-ee-koe)
I can't stand... / I hate... (literally "I have the horror of...")	Ho l'orrore di... (o lo-roar-ay dee)
I can't stand flying! / I hate flying!	Ho l'orrore di volare! (o lo-roar-ay dee vol-are-ay)

I can't stand living with my in-laws / I hate living with my in-laws.	Ho l'orrore di abitare con i miei suoceri. (o lo-roar-ay dee ab-it-are-ay kon ee mee-ay soo-o-chair-ee)
We can't stand eating with my parents / We hate eating with my parents.	Abbiamo l'orrore di mangiare con i miei genitori. (ab-ee-arm-oh lo-roar-ay dee mange-are-ay kon ee mee-ay jen-ee-tore-ee)
She can't stand working here / She hates working here.	Lei ha l'orrore di lavorare qui. (lay a lo-roar-ay dee lavo-or-are-ay kwee)
I was	Ero (air-oh)
solitary	solitario (sol-eet-are-ee-oh)
contrary	contrario (kon-trar-ee-oh)
ordinary	ordinario (or-deen-are-ee-oh)
I was ordinary.	Ero ordinario. (air-oh or-deen-are-ee-oh)
I was about to… / I was just about to… (literally "I stayed for…")	Stavo per… (starve-oh pair)
I was about to prepare the dinner / I was just about to prepare the dinner.	Stavo per preparare la cena. (starve-oh pair pray-par-are-ay la chain-er)
I was about to pay the bill.	Stavo per pagare il conto. (starve-oh pair pag-are-ay eel kon-toe)
I was just about to book a table.	Stavo per prenotare un tavolo. (starve-oh pair pray-note-are-ay oon tav-oh-loe)
You called me / You did call me / You have called me. (formal)	Mi ha chiamato. (mee a kee-am-art-oh)
You called me / You did call me / You have called me. (informal)	Mi hai chiamato. (mee eye kee-am-art-oh)
when	quando (kwan-doe)
I was just about to book a taxi when you called me. Really!	Stavo per prenotare un taxi quando mi hai chiamato. Veramente! (starve-oh pair pray-note-are-ay oon taxi kwan-doe mee eye kee-am-art-oh. ve-ra-men-tay)

I was about to leave when the telephone rang.	Stavo per partire quando il telefono ha squillato. (starve-oh pair part-ear-ray kwan-doe eel tel-off-on-oh a skwee-lar-toe
I was just about to phone you when you knocked at the door. (informal)	Stavo per telefonarti quando hai bussato alla porta. (starve-oh pair tel-ef-own-are-tee kwan-doe eye boos-art-oh al-la port-er)
I was just about to order a taxi when it started to rain.	Stavo per ordinare un taxi quando ha cominciato a piovere. (starve-oh pair or-din-are-ay oon taxi kwan-doe a kom-in-chart-oh a pee-oh-vair-ay)
so (extremely, very)	così (koh-see)
I was so romantic.	Ero così romantico. (air-oh koh-zee roe-man-teek-oh)
I was so illogical.	Ero così illogico. (air-oh koh-zee ee-lodge-eek-oh)
is	è (ay)
Mario is romantic.	Mario è romantico. (ma-ree-oh ay roe-man-teek-oh)
Maria is romantic.	Maria è romantica. (ma-ree-ah ay roe-man-teek-a)
I am	Sono (son-oh)
arrived	arrivato / arrivata (a-reev-art-oh / a-reev-art-a)
I have arrived / I arrived / I did arrive. (said by a man / boy)	Sono arrivato. (son-oh a-reev-art-oh)
I have arrived / I arrived / I did arrive. (said by a woman / girl)	Sono arrivata. (son-oh a-reev-art-a)
gone	andato / andata (and-art-oh / and-art-a)
I have gone / I went / I did go. (said by a man / boy)	Sono andato. (son-oh and-art-oh)
I have gone / I went / I did go. (said by a woman / girl)	Sono andata. (son-oh and-art-oh)
You are (formal)	È (ay)

You have gone / You went / You did go. (said to a man / boy) – (formal)	È andato. (ay and-art-oh)
You have gone / You went / You did go. (said to a woman / girl) – (formal)	È andata. (ay and-art-oh)
You have arrived / You arrived / You did arrive. (said to a man / boy) – (formal)	È arrivato. (ay a-reev-art-oh)
You have arrived / You arrived / You did arrive. (said to a woman / girl) – (formal)	È arrivata. (ay a-reev-art-a)
You are (informal)	Sei (say)
You have arrived / You arrived / You did arrive. (said to a man / boy) – (informal)	Sei arrivato. (say a-reev-art-oh)
You have arrived / You arrived / You did arrive. (said to a woman / girl) – (informal)	Sei arrivata. (say a-reev-art-a)
I'm sorry.	Mi dispiace. (mee dis-pee-arch-ey)
a little / a bit	un po' (oon po)
I was a little distracted.	Ero un po' distratto / distratta. (air-oh oon po dee-stra-toe / dee-stra-ta)
I was in the middle of…	Stavo… (starve-oh)
I'm sorry, I was in the middle of eating when you arrived. (informal)	Mi dispiace, stavo mangiando quando sei arrivato / arrivata. (mee dis-pee-arch-ey, starve-oh mange-and-oh kwan-doe say a-reev-art-oh / a-reev-art-a)
I'm sorry, I was in the middle of preparing dinner when you arrived, so I was a bit distracted. (informal)	Mi dispiace, stavo preparando la cena quando sei arrivato / arrivata, quindi ero un po' distratto / distratta. (mee dis-pee-arch-ey, starve-oh pray-par-ay la chain-er kwan-doe say a-reev-art-oh / a-reev-art-a, kwin-dee air-oh oon po dee-stra-toe / dee-stra-ta)

I was in the middle of studying when my mother arrived.	Stavo studiando quando mia madre è arrivata. (starve-oh stood-ee-and-oh kwan-doe mee-a mard-re ay a-reev-art-a)
I was in the middle of cooking when you phoned me.	Stavo cucinando quando mi hai telefonato. (starve-oh koo-cheen-an-doe kwan-doe mee eye tay-lay-fone-art-oh)
I was in the middle of having dinner when your email arrived.	Stavo cenando quando la tua e-mail è arrivata. (starve-oh chen-an-deo kwan-doe la too-a ee-mail ay a-reev-art-a)
July	luglio (lool-yoh)
this July	questo luglio (kwest-oh lool-yoh)
I visited Rome this July / I have visited Rome this July / I did visit Rome this July.	Ho visitato Roma questo luglio. (o visit-art-oh roam-er kwest-oh lool-yoh)
I'm planning to visit Rome this July.	Ho intenzione di visitare Roma questo luglio. (o in-ten-tzee-oh-nay dee visit-are-ay roam-er kwest-oh lool-yoh)
I'm moving (literally "Myself I transfer")	Mi trasferisco (mee tras-fur-ees-koh)
I'm moving to Italy this September.	Mi trasferisco in Italia questo settembre. (mee tras-fur-ees-koh een eet-al-yer kwest-oh se-tem-bray)
because of you (informal)	per causa tua (pair kow-zer too-er)
thanks to...	grazie a... (grats-ee-ey)
Thanks to me!	Grazie a me! (grats-ee-ey a mey)
I'm moving to Italy this July because of you! (informal)	Mi trasferisco in Italia questo luglio per causa tua! (mee tras-fur-ees-koh een eet-al-yer kwest-oh lool-yoh a roam-er pair kow-zer too-er)
Do you want? (literally "Want you?") – (informal)	Vuoi? (vwoy)
Do you want to prepare the dinner this evening? (informal)	Vuoi preparare la cena questa sera? (vwoy pray-par-are-ay la chain-er kwest-er sair-er)

Do you want to eat something? (informal)	Vuoi mangiare qualcosa? (vwoy mange-are-ay kwal-koe-zer)
You want (informal)	Vuoi (vwoy)
to say	dire (dear-ay)
You mean (literally "You want to say") – (informal)	Vuoi dire (vwoy dear-ay)
I'm moving to Italy this July because of you! (informal)	Mi trasferisco in Italia questo luglio per causa tua! (mee tras-fur-ees-koh een eet-al-yer kwest-oh lool-yoh a roam-er pair kow-zer too-er)
Because of me? You mean *thanks* to me! (informal)	*Per causa* mia? Vuoi dire *grazie* a me! (pair kow-zer mee-er vwoy dear-ay grats-ee-ey a mey)
actually / in fact	in realtà (een ray-al-ta)
I too / I also	anch'io (arnk-ee-o)
Actually, I'm moving to Florence too.	In realtà, anch'io mi trasferisco a Firenze. (een ray-al-ta, arnk-ee-o mee tras-fur-ees-koh a fee-rents-ey)
Actually, I'm also moving to Italy next month.	In realtà, anch'io mi trasferisco in Italia il mese prossimo. (een ray-al-ta, arnk-ee-o mee tras-fur-ees-koh een eet-al-yer eel may-zay pross-ee-moe)
Actually, I'm also going to Rome next year.	In realtà, anch'io vado a Roma l'anno prossimo. (een ray-al-ta, arnk-ee-o var-doe a roam-er lan-oh pross-ee-moe)

And it's done! Take a break now before you dive into the final chapter!

The Great Word Robbery

Since the very beginning of the book, I've been giving you examples of how you can rapidly build up your Italian vocabulary by stealing and converting words from English. Really though, what I've shown you so far has only been the tip of that enormous iceberg I mentioned in the Introduction.

I'm now going to give you a far more comprehensive list of word endings that you can use to create thousands of words in Italian.

Once you've had a read through them, I recommend that you try coming up with a few more examples for each, and saying them out loud. The more you do this the more you will find yourself able to apply the various conversion techniques between English and Italian almost instinctively.

So, here is the list – it will be your single greatest aid in increasing your Italian vocabulary:

Words ending in... in English	Usually become... in Italian	Examples
ation	azione	decorazione preparazione trasformazione **(1250)**
ic/ical	ico	politico tipico drammatico **(750)**
ary	ario	primario salario volontario **(400)**
ous	oso	curioso furioso dubbioso **(700)**

Words ending in... in English	Usually become... in Italian	Examples
ade	ata	barricata parata cascata (150)
ude	udine	gratitudine solitudine altitudine (100)
ure	ura	natura cultura caricatura (300)
ible	ibile	terribile possibile visibile (800)
able	abile	abile usabile probabile (800)
ant	ante	importante elegante galante (700)
ent	ente	presidente cliente recente (700)
id	ido	vivido rapido timido (300)

Words ending in... in English	Usually become... in Italian	Examples
sm	smo	pessimismo pacifismo sarcasmo **(800)**
ty	tà	realtà atrocità agilità **(1500)**
or	ore	pastore aviatore curatore **(800)**
ist	ista	artista pianista lista **(1000)**
al	ale	brutale canale vitale **(200)**
ive	ivo	creativo evasivo corrosivo **(750)**

Word Robbery Total : 12,000

Wow, 12,000 English words that have close relatives in Italian. Not too shabby in my opinion.

I recommend returning to the list every so often to practise stealing words via the conversion techniques. Try to come up with a couple of examples for each and then check them in a dictionary as a way to learn any exceptions to the rules given above.

CHAPTER 8

When you talk about Rome,
you're so enthusiastic.

When you talk about Rome, you're so enthusiastic.

Well, you've worked through seven chapters to get to this point. I think it's time to see what you're capable of saying based on all you've learnt with the book.

You are now going to build up to a much longer dialogue than you've done previously *but* much of what you're using will already be familiar to you.

I am sure that you can definitely do this, so let's begin.

What is "I have visited", "I visited", "I did visit"?

Ho visitato
(*o* visit-art-oh)

How about "I have reserved / booked", "I reserved / booked", "I did reserve / book"?

Ho prenotato
(*o* pray no-tart-oh)

"I have prepared", "I prepared", "I did prepare"?

Ho preparato
(*o* prep-are-art-oh)

"I have ordered", "I ordered", "I did order"?

Ho ordinato
(*o* or-din-art-oh)

"I have paid", "I paid", I did pay"?

Ho pagato
(*o* pag-art-oh)

"I have spent", "I spent", "I did spend"?

Ho passato
(*o* pass-art-oh)

How would you say "I spent the weekend in Italy"?

Ho passato il weekend in Italia.
(*o pass-art-oh eel weekend een eet-al-yer*)

And how would you say "it was" in Italian?

Era
(*air-ah*)

And so how would you say "it was fantastic"?

Era fantastico.
(*air-ah fan-tass-teek-oh*)

And what was the word for "and" in Italian?

(*ay*)

Alright, how would you say "I spent the weekend in Italy – and wow, the weather was fantastic"?

Ho passato il weekend in Italia – e wow, il tempo era fantastico.
(*o pass-art-oh eel weekend een eet-al-yer ay wow, eel-tem-poe air-ah fan-tass-teek-oh*)

And how would you say "I'm planning to..." in Italian?

Ho intenzione di...
(*o in-ten-tzee-oh-nay dee*)

So, how would you say "I'm planning to go back to Rome in May"?

Ho intenzione di ritornare a Roma a maggio.
(*o in-ten-tzee-oh-nay dee ri-torn-are-ay a roam-er a madge-oh*)

Now, let's put those two bits together and say "I spent the weekend in Italy – and wow, the weather was fantastic. I'm planning to go back to Rome in May":

Ho passato il weekend in Italia – e wow, il tempo era fantastico. Ho intenzione di ritornare a Roma a maggio.
(*o pass-art-oh eel weekend een eet-al-yer ay wow, eel-tem-poe air-ah fan-tass-teek-oh. o in-ten-tzee-oh-nay dee ri-torn-are-ay a roam-er a madge-oh*)

Now again, what is "I have"?

Ho
(*o*)

And "he has"?

Lui ha
(*loo-ee a*)

"She has"?

Lei ha
(*lay a*)

"We have"?

Abbiamo
(*ab-ee-arm-oh*)

"They have"?

Loro hanno
(*lo-roe an-oh*)

"You have" (formal)?

Ha
(a)

"You have" (informal)?

Hai
(eye)

So, how would you say "you are planning to…" (informal)?

Hai intenzione di…
(eye in-ten-tzee-oh-nay dee)

And how would you say "you're scared of…" (informal)?

Hai paura di…
(eye pow-oo-rer dee)

How about "you're scared of flying" (informal)?

Hai paura di volare.
(eye pow-oo-rer dee vol-are-ay)

What is "but"?

ma
(mu)

With this in mind, how would you say "But you're scared of flying!"?

Ma hai paura di volare!
(mu eye pow-oo-rer dee vol-are-ay)

What is "to take"?

prendere
(pren-de-rey)

So, how would you say "I'm planning to take the Eurostar"?

Ho intenzione di prendere l'Eurostar.
(o in-ten-tzee-oh-nay dee pren-de-rey lay-oo-roe-star)

What is "so" (meaning "therefore") in Italian?

quindi
(kwin-dee)

So, how would you say "So I'm planning to take the Eurostar"?

Quindi ho intenzione di prendere l'Eurostar.
(kwin-dee o in-ten-tzee-oh-nay dee pren-de-rey lay-oo-roe-star)

And again, what is "I'm planning to..."?

Ho intenzione di...
(o in-ten-tzee-oh-nay dee)

And what is "I'm scared of"?

Ho paura di...
(o pow-oo-rer dee)

What about "I can't stand..."?

Ho l'orrore di...
(o lo-roar-ay dee)

So, how would you say "I can't stand taking the Eurostar"?

Ho l'orrore di prendere l'Eurostar.
(o lo-roar-ay dee pren-de-rey lay-oo-roe-star)

What is "really"?

veramente
(ve-ra-men-tay)

So, how would you say "Really? I can't stand taking the Eurostar!"

Veramente? Ho l'orrore di prendere l'Eurostar!
(ve-ra-men-tay o lo-roar-ay dee pren-de-rey lay-oo-roe-star)

What is "I need..."?

Ho bisogno di...
(o beez-on-yoe dee)

And how would you say "he needs..." (literally "he has need of...")?

Lui ha bisogno di...
(loo-ee a beez-on-yoe dee)

And "she needs..." (literally "she has need of...")?

Lei ha bisogno di...
(lay a beez-on-yoe dee)

How about "we need..."?

Abbiamo bisogno di...
(ab-ee-arm-oh beez-on-yoe dee)

And "they need..."?

Loro hanno bisogno di...
(lo-roe an-oh beez-on-yoe dee)

What about "you need..." (formal)?

Ha bisogno di...
(a beez-on-yoe dee)

And "you need..." (informal)?

Hai bisogno di...
(*eye beez-on-yoe dee*)

Okay, how would you say "you need help, mate!" (informal)?

Hai bisogno di aiuto, amico!
(*eye bisogno di eye-oot-oh am-ee-koe*)

Of course, you might not want to always call someone "mate." You may just want to call them by their names.

So, how would you say "you need help, Mario!"?

Hai bisogno di aiuto, Mario!
(*eye bisogno di eye-oot-oh, ma-ree-oh*)

And what about, "you need help, Maria!"?

Hai bisogno di aiuto, Maria!
(*eye bisogno di eye-oot-oh, ma-ree-ah*)

And again, What is "is"?

è
(ay)

And so how would you say "the Eurostar is fantastic"?

L'Eurostar è fantastico.
(lay-*oo*-roe-star ay fan-tass-teek-oh)

What is "I was just about to…"?

Stavo per…
(starve-oh pair)

And "I was just about to book a table"?

Stavo per prenotare un tavolo.
(starve-oh pair pray-note-are-ay *oon* tav-oh-loe)

How about "I was just about to book a taxi"?

Stavo per prenotare un taxi.
(starve-oh pair pray-note-are-ay *oon* taxi)

"I was just about to book a room"?

Stavo per prenotare una camera.
(starve-oh pair pray-note-are-ay *oon*-a cam-air-a)

"A ticket" in Italian is:

un biglietto
(*oon* bee-lye-toe)

How would you say "I was just about to book a ticket"?

Stavo per prenotare un biglietto.
(starve-oh pair pray-note-are-ay *oon* bee-lye-toe)

What is the word for "and"?

e
(ay)

So how would you say "...and I was just about to book a ticket"?

...e stavo per prenotare un biglietto
(ay starve-oh pair pray-note-are-ay oon bee-lye-toe)

And how you would you say "I arrived" in Italian?

Sono arrivato / arrivata.
(son-oh a-reev-art-oh / a-reev-art-a)

How about "you arrived" (informal)?

Sei arrivato / arrivata.
(say a-reev-art-oh / a-reev-art-a)

And so, how would you say "...when you arrived" (informal)?

...quando sei arrivato / arrivata
(kwan-doe say a-reev-art-oh / a-reev-art-a)

Put these various parts together now and say "...and I was just about to book a ticket when you arrived.":

...e stavo per prenotare un biglietto quando sei arrivato / arrivata.
(ay starve-oh pair pray-note-are-ay oon bee-lye-toe kwan-doe say
a-reev-art-oh / a-reev-art-a)

Now let's put both this and the other parts that came before it together.

Taking your time and say: "You need help, Mario! The Eurostar is fantastic and I was just about to book a ticket when you arrived."

Hai bisogno di aiuto, Mario! l'Eurostar è fantastico e stavo per prenotare un biglietto quando sei arrivato.
(eye bisogno di eye-oot-oh ma-ree-oh. lay-oo-roe-star ay fan-tass-teek-oh
ay starve-oh pair pray-note-are-ay oon bee-lye-toe kwan-doe say
a-reev-art-oh)

Notice how, as we're speaking to Mario, arrived can only be "arrivato."

Let's try this again but this time talking to a woman. Say, "You need help, Maria! The Eurostar is fantastic and I was just about to book a ticket when you arrived."

Hai bisogno di aiuto, Maria! l'Eurostar è fantastico e stavo per prenotare un biglietto quando sei arrivata.
(eye bisogno di eye-oot-oh ma-ree-ah. lay-oo-roe-star ay fan-tass-teek-oh ay starve-oh pair pray-note-are-ay oon bee-lye-toe kwan-doe say a-reev-art-a)

Now, how would someone say "Really?" in response to that?

Veramente?
(ve-ra-men-tay)

And how would you say "I was in the middle of booking"?

Stavo prenotando
(starve-oh pray-note-and-oh)

So, how would you say "I was in the middle of booking a ticket"?

Stavo prenotando un biglietto.
(starve-oh pray-note-and-oh oon bee-lye-toe)

And how would you say "...when you knocked at the door"?

...quando hai bussato alla porta
(kwan-doe eye boos-art-oh al-la port-er)

Let's now combine these elements and say "I was in the middle of booking a ticket when you knocked at the door.":

Stavo prenotando un biglietto quando hai bussato alla porta.
(starve-oh pray-note-and-oh oon bee-lye-toe kwan-doe eye boos-art-oh al-la port-er)

How would someone reply to this saying "oh, sorry"?

Oh, mi dispiace.
(oh, mee dis-pee-arch-ey)

What is "I feel like…" or "I fancy…"?

Ho voglia di…
(o vol-ya dee)

How about "I feel like visiting Rome"?

Ho voglia di visitare Roma.
(o vol-ya dee visit-are-ay roam-er)

What is "I also" (literally "also I") in Italian?

anch'io
(arnk-ee-o)

So, how would you say "I also feel like visiting Rome"?

Anch'io ho voglia di visitare Roma.
(arnk-ee-o o vol-ya dee visit-are-ay roam-er)

What is "actually" or "in fact" in Italian?

in realtà
(een ray-al-ta)

If you wanted to give a fuller answer, how would you say "Oh, sorry. Actually, I also feel like visiting Rome."?

Oh, mi dispiace. In realtà, anch'io ho voglia di visitare Roma.
(oh, mee dis-pee-arch-ey. een ray-al-ta arnk-ee-o o vol-ya dee visit-are-ay roam-er)

How would someone reply to that by saying "Really?"

Veramente?
(ve-ra-men-tay)

What is "I'm planning to" (literally "I have intention of…")?

Ho intenzione di…
(o in-ten-tzee-oh-nay dee)

So, if "ho intenzione di..." means literally "I have intention of...", which of those words means "of"?

di
(dee)

What is "to speak" or "to talk" in Italian?

parlare
(par-lar-ay)

"You speak" or "you talk" (informal) in Italian is:

parli
(par-lee)

To say "you speak about" or "you talk about" in Italian, you will literally say "you speak of" or "you talk of".

So how would you say "you talk about" (informal) – (literally "you speak of / you talk of")?

parli di
(par-lee dee)

Now how do you say "you talk about Rome" (informal)?

Parli di Roma.
(par-lee dee roam-er)

How about "when you talk about Rome" (informal)?

quando parli di Roma
(kon par-lee dee roam-er)

What is "you are" (informal)?

Sei
(say)

And what is "enthusiastic"?

entusiasta[7]
(en-tooze-ee-ast-a)

And what is "so" (in the sense of "extremely" or "very")?

così
(koh-zee)

How would you say "you are so enthusiastic" (informal)?

Sei così entusiasta.
(say koh-zee en-tooze-ee-ast-a)

If you want to reply to something you feel is a compliment you can, of course, say "thank you". Many people will be already familiar with the Italian word for "thank you", which is:

grazie
(grats-ee-ey)

And if you want to make that more emphatic, you can say "wow, thank you!"

So, say that now, "wow, thank you!"

Wow, grazie!
(wow grats-ee-ey)

And once again, what is "you speak" or "you talk" (informal) in Italian?

parli
(par-lee)

And how would you say "you speak about" or "you talk about" (informal) – (literally "you speak of / you talk of ")?

parli di
(par-lee dee)

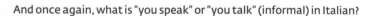

---

7   And remember, "enthusiastic" in Italian remains "entusiasta", whether you're describing a man or a woman!

And so how would you you say "you talk about Rome" (informal)?

parli di Roma
(par-lee dee roam-er)

And what about "when you talk about Rome" (informal)?

quando parli di Roma
(kon par-lee dee roam-er)

And again, how would you say "you are so enthusiastic" (informal)?

sei così entusiasta.
(say koh-zee en-tooze-ee-ast-a)

Putting this all together, now say "When you talk about Rome you are so enthusiastic.":

Quando parli di Roma sei così entusiasta.
(kwin-dee kon par-lee dee roam-er say koh-zee en-tooze-ee-ast-a)

How would the person you were talking to reply "Wow, thanks!"?

Wow, grazie!
(wow, grats-ee-ey)

If, by your enthusiasm, you actually managed to persuade someone that they also wanted to go to Rome, they might say "Wow, thanks, let's go then!"
"Let's go!" or "Let's go then!" is:

Andiamo!
(and-ee-arm-oh)

So, finally, how would you say "Wow, thanks! Let's go then!"?

Wow, grazie! Andiamo!
(wow grats-ee-ey. and-ee-arm-oh)

Alright, I think it's time for you to have a crack at the long dialogue I mentioned at the beginning of the chapter.

Try going through it, slowly the first couple of times and then, once you feel confident enough, see if you can get to the point where you can construct the entire dialogue without needing to pause. It will take a fair amount of practice but, every time you go through it, it will greatly benefit your Italian.

As you will already be finding, I hope, the more you practise constructing these sentences, the more natural and fluent you will sound.

Are you ready then? Take your time and off you go with the final dialogue:

I spent the weekend in Italy – and wow, the weather was fantastic. I'm planning to go back to Rome in May.
Ho passato il weekend in Italia – e wow, il tempo era fantastico. Ho intenzione di ritornare a Roma a maggio.
(o pass-art-oh eel weekend een eet-al-yer ay wow, eel-tem-poe air-ah fan-tass-teek-oh. o in-ten-tzee-oh-nay dee ri-torn-are-ay a roam-er a madge-oh)

But you're scared of flying!
Ma hai paura di volare!
(mu eye pow-oo-rer dee vol-are-ay)

Yes, so I'm planning to take the Eurostar.
Sì, quindi ho intenzione di prendere l'Eurostar.
(see, kwin-dee o in-ten-tzee-oh-nay dee pren-de-rey lay-oo-roe-star)

Really? I can't stand taking the Eurostar.
Veramente? Ho l'orrore di prendere l'Eurostar!
(ve-ra-men-tay o lo-roar-ay dee pren-de-rey lay-oo-roe-star)

You need help, Mario / Maria! The Eurostar is fantastic and I was just about to book a ticket when you arrived.
Hai bisogno di aiuto Mario / Maria! L'Eurostar è fantastico e stavo per prenotare un biglietto quando sei arrivato / arrivata.
(eye bisogno di eye-oot-oh ma-ree-oh / ma-ree-ah. lay-oo-roe-star ay fan-tass-teek-oh ay starve-oh pair pray-note-are-ay oon bee-lye-toe kwan-doe say a-reev-art-oh / a-reev-art-a)

Really?
Veramente?
(ve-ra-men-tay)

Yes, I was in the middle of booking a ticket when you knocked at the door.
Sì, stavo prenotando un biglietto quando hai bussato alla porta.
(see, starve-oh pray-note-and-oh oon bee-lye-toe kwan-doe eye boos-art-oh al-la port-er)

Oh, sorry. Actually, I also feel like visiting Rome.
Oh, mi dispiace. In realtà, anch'io ho voglia di visitare Roma.
(oh, mee dis-pee-arch-ey. een ray-al-ta, arnk-ee-o o vol-ya dee visit-are-ay roam-er)

Really?
Veramente?
(ve-ra-men-tay)

Yes – because of you.
Sì, per causa tua.
(see, pair kow-zer too-er)

Because of me? Really?
Per causa mia? Veramente?
(pair kow-zer mee-er? ve-ra-men-tay)

Yes, when you talk about Rome you're so enthusiastic.
Sì, quando parli di Roma sei così entusiasta.
(see, kwan-doe par-lee dee roam-er say koh-zee en-tooze-ee-ast-a)

Wow, thanks! Let's go then!
Wow, grazie! Andiamo!
(wow grats-ee-ey. and-ee-arm-oh)

Well, this is your final checklist. Unlike the ones that came before it, however, you are not finished with this one until you can go the whole way through it without making a single mistake.

This doesn't mean that making mistakes when you go through it is a bad thing. It's just that I want you to return to it multiple times so that going through the list becomes so easy that you can do it without making a single error.

When you can, it means you have really learnt what I wanted to teach you in these pages.

Now, get to it!

il weekend (eel weekend)	the weekend
romantico (roe-man-teek-oh)	romantic
fantastico (fan-tass-teek-oh)	fantastic
politico (pol-ee-teek-oh)	political
illogico (ee-lodge-eek-oh)	illogical
entusiasta (en-tooze-ee-ast-a)	enthusiastic
Ho (o)	I have
visitato (visit-art-oh)	visited
Ho visitato (o visit-art-oh)	I have visited / I visited / I did visit
Roma (roam-er)	Rome
Napoli (nap-oh-lee)	Naples
Ho visitato Napoli. (o visit-art-oh nap-oh-lee)	I have visited Naples / I visited Naples / I did visit Naples.
passato (pass-art-oh)	spent
Ho passato (o pass-art-oh)	I have spent / I spent / I did spend
Ha (a)	You have
Ha passato (a pass-art-oh)	You have spent / You spent / You did spend
Abbiamo (ab-ee-arm-oh)	We have

Abbiamo passato (ab-ee-arm-oh pass-art-oh)	We have spent / We spent / We did spend
settembre (se-tem-bray)	September
il Natale (eel nat-arl-ay)	Christmas
a Roma (a roam-er)	in Rome
in Italia (een eet-al-yer)	in Italy
in Svizzera (een zvee-tser-er)	in Switzerland
Abbiamo passato il Natale in Svizzera. (ab-ee-arm-oh pass-art-oh eel nat-arl-ay een zvee-tser-er)	We have spent Christmas in Switzerland / We spent Christmas in Switzerland / We did spend Christmas in Switzerland.
Ha passato settembre in Italia. (a pass-art-oh se-tem-bray con eet-al-yer)	You have spent September in Italy / You spent September in Italy / You did spend September in Italy.
e (ay)	and
Era (air-ah)	It was
Era fantastico. (air-ah fan-tass-teek-oh)	It was fantastic.
Il tempo era fantastico. (eel-tem-poe air-ah fan-tass-teek-oh)	The weather was fantastic.
Ho passato il weekend a Roma – e wow, il tempo era fantastico. (o pass-art-oh eel weekend a roam-er ay wow, eel-tem-poe air-ah fan-tass-teek-oh)	I spent the weekend in Rome – and wow, the weather was fantastic.
preparazione (prep-are-atz-ee-oh-nay)	preparation
preparato (pray-par-ato)	prepared
prenotazione (pray-no-tatz-ee-oh-nay)	reservation
prenotato (pray-no-tart-oh)	reserved / booked
ordinato (or-din-art-oh)	ordered
pagato (pag-art-oh)	paid
fatto (fat-oh)	done

il conto (eel kon-toe)	the bill
la cena (la chain-er)	the dinner
il caffè (eel ka-fe)	the coffee
un tavolo (oon tav-oh-loe)	a table
una camera (oon-a cam-air-a)	a room
un taxi (oon taxi)	a taxi
Ho preparato la cena. (o prep-are-art-oh la chain-er)	I have prepared the dinner / I prepared the dinner / I did prepare the dinner.
Ho ordinato il caffè per la cena. (o or-din-art-oh eel ka-fe pair la chain-er)	I have ordered coffee for dinner / I ordered coffee for dinner / I did order coffee for dinner.
Ho prenotato un tavolo per Lei. (o pray-no-tart-oh oon tav-oh-loe pair lay)	I have booked a table for you / I booked a table for you / I did book a table for you.
Lei ha (lay a)	She has
Lei ha prenotato un tavolo per questa sera. (lay a pray-no-tart-oh oon tav-oh-loe pair kwest-er sair-er)	She has booked / reserved a table for this evening – She booked / reserved a table for this evening – She did book / reserve a table for this evening.
Lui ha (loo-ee a)	He has
Lui ha prenotato una camera per due persone. (loo-ee a pray-no-tart-oh oon-a cam-air-a pair doo-ay pair-soan-ay)	He has booked / reserved a room for two people – He booked / reserved a room for two people – He did book / reserve a room for two people.
Abbiamo prenotato un taxi per Lei. (ab-ee-arm-oh pray-no-tart-oh oon taxi pair lay)	We have booked a taxi for you / We booked a taxi for you / We did book a taxi for you.
Abbiamo pagato il conto. (ab-ee-arm-oh pag-art-oh eel kon-toe)	We paid the bill / We have paid the bill / We did pay the bill.
Che cosa? (ke koe-ser)	What? / What thing?
Che cosa ha preparato? (ke koe-ser a prep-are-art-oh)	What have you prepared? / What did you prepare? (literally "What thing you have prepared?")

Che cosa ha fatto? (ke koe-ser a fat-oh)	What have you done? / What did you do? (literally "What thing you have done?")
Ho prenotato un tavolo, ordinato la cena e poi pagato il conto. Che cosa ha fatto? (o pray-no-tart-oh oon tav-oh-loe, or-din-art-oh la chain-er ey poy pag-art-oh eel kon-toe. ke koe-ser a fat-oh)	I booked a table, ordered dinner and then paid the bill. What did you do?
Ho intenzione di... (o in-ten-tzee-oh-nay dee)	I'm planning to... (literally "I have intention of...")
Ho intenzione di ritornare in Italia a maggio. (o in-ten-tzee-oh-nay dee ri-torn-are-ay een eet-al-yer a madge-oh)	I'm planning to go back to Italy in May.
Ho paura di... (o pow-oo-rer dee)	I'm scared of... (literally "I have fear of...")
Ho paura di ritornare in Italia a settembre. (o pow-oo-rer dee ri-torn-are-ay een eet-al-yer a se-tem-bray)	I'm scared of going back to Italy in September.
Veramente? (ve-ra-men-tay)	Really?
quindi (kwin-dee)	so (therefore)
ma (mu)	but
Ho voglia di... (o vol-ya dee)	I feel like... / I fancy... (literally "I have want of...")
Sì, ho voglia di ritornare a Roma ma ho paura di volare, quindi ho intenzione di prendere l'Eurostar. (see, o vol-ya dee ri-torn-are-ay a roam-er mu o pow-oo-rer dee vol-are-ay, kwin-dee o in-ten-tzee-oh-nay dee pren-de-rey lay-oo-roe-star)	Yes, I feel like / fancy going back to Rome but I'm scared of flying, so I'm planning to take the Eurostar.
Ho voglia di comprare qualcosa questa mattina. (o vol-ya dee com-prar-ay kwal-koe-zer kwest-er mat-een-er	I feel like / fancy buying something this morning.

Lui ha voglia di leggere qualcosa questo pomeriggio. (loo-ee a vol-ya dee ledge-er-ay kwal-koe-zer kwest-oh pom-air-idge-oh)	He feels like / fancies reading something this afternoon.
Loro hanno (lo-roe an-oh)	They have
Loro hanno voglia di mangiare qualcosa questa sera. (lo-roe an-oh vol-ya dee mange-are-ay kwal-koe-zer kwest-er sair-er)	They feel like / fancy eating something this evening.
Ho bisogno di… (o beez-on-yoe dee)	I need… (literally "I have need of…")
Ho bisogno di parlare italiano. (o beez-on-yoe dee par-lar-ay eet-al-ee-arn-oh)	I need to speak Italian.
Ho bisogno di un taxi. (o beez-on-yoe dee oon taxi)	I need a taxi.
Ho bisogno di una camera. (o beez-on-yoe dee oon-a cam-air-a)	I need a room.
Ho bisogno di aiuto. (o bisogno di eye-oot-oh)	I need help.
Hai bisogno di aiuto, amico! (eye bisogno di eye-oot-oh am-ee-koe)	You need help, mate!
Ho l'orrore di… (o lo-roar-ay dee)	I can't stand… / I hate… (literally "I have the horror of…")
Ho l'orrore di volare! (o lo-roar-ay dee vol-are-ay)	I can't stand flying! / I hate flying!
Ho l'orrore di abitare con i miei suoceri. (o lo-roar-ay dee ab-it-are-ay kon ee mee-ay soo-o-chair-ee)	I can't stand living with my in-laws / I hate living with my in-laws.
Abbiamo l'orrore di mangiare con i miei genitori. (ab-ee-arm-oh lo-roar-ay dee mange-are-ay kon ee mee-ay jen-ee-tore-ee)	We can't stand eating with my parents / We hate eating with my parents.
Lei ha l'orrore di lavorare qui. (lay a lo-roar-ay dee lavo-or-are-ay kwee)	She can't stand working here / She hates working here.
Ero (air-oh)	I was
solitario (sol-eet-are-ee-oh)	solitary

contrario (kon-trar-ee-oh)	contrary
ordinario (or-deen-are-ee-oh)	ordinary
Ero ordinario. (air-oh or-deen-are-ee-oh)	I was ordinary.
Stavo per... (starve-oh pair)	I was about to... / I was just about to... (literally "I stayed for...")
Stavo per preparare la cena. (starve-oh pair pray-par-are-ay la chain-er)	I was about to prepare the dinner / I was just about to prepare the dinner.
Stavo per pagare il conto. (starve-oh pair pag-are-ay eel kon-toe)	I was about to pay the bill.
Stavo per prenotare un tavolo. (starve-oh pair pray-note-are-ay oon tav-oh-loe)	I was just about to book a table.
Mi ha chiamato. (mee a kee-am-art-oh)	You called me / You did call me / You have called me. (formal)
Mi hai chiamato. (mee eye kee-am-art-oh)	You called me / You did call me / You have called me. (informal)
quando (kwan-doe)	when
Stavo per prenotare un taxi quando mi hai chiamato. Veramente! (starve-oh pair pray-note-are-ay oon taxi kwan-doe mee eye kee-am-art-oh. ve-ra-men-tay)	I was just about to book a taxi when you called me. Really!
Stavo per partire quando il telefono ha squillato. (starve-oh pair part-ear-ray kwan-doe eel tel-off-on-oh a skwee-lar-toe	I was about to leave when the telephone rang.
Stavo per telefonarti quando hai bussato alla porta. (starve-oh pair tel-ef-own-are-tee kwan-doe eye boos-art-oh al-la port-er)	I was just about to phone you when you knocked at the door. (informal)
Stavo per ordinare un taxi quando ha cominciato a piovere. (starve-oh pair or-din-are-ay oon taxi kwan-doe a kom-in-chart-oh a pee-oh-vair-ay)	I was just about to order a taxi when it started to rain.

così (koh-see)	so (extremely, very)
Ero così romantico. (air-oh koh-zee roe-man-teek-oh)	I was so romantic.
Ero così illogico. (air-oh koh-zee ee-lodge-eek-oh)	I was so illogical.
è (ay)	is
Mario è romantico. (ma-ree-oh ay roe-man-teek-oh)	Mario is romantic.
Maria è romantica. (ma-ree-ah ay roe-man-teek-a)	Maria is romantic.
Sono (son-oh)	I am
arrivato / arrivata (a-reev-art-oh / a-reev-art-a)	arrived
Sono arrivato. (son-oh a-reev-art-oh)	I have arrived / I arrived / I did arrive. (said by a man / boy)
Sono arrivata. (son-oh a-reev-art-a)	I have arrived / I arrived / I did arrive. (said by a woman / girl)
andato / andata (and-art-oh / and-art-a)	gone
Sono andato. (son-oh and-art-oh)	I have gone / I went / I did go. (said by a man / boy)
Sono andata. (son-oh and-art-a)	I have gone / I went / I did go. (said by a woman / girl)
È (ay)	You are (formal)
È andato. (ay and-art-oh)	You have gone / You went / You did go. (said to a man / boy) – (formal)
È andata. (ay and-art-a)	You have gone / You went / You did go. (said to a woman / girl) – (formal)
È arrivato. (ay a-reev-art-oh)	You have arrived / You arrived / You did arrive. (said to a man / boy) – (formal)
È arrivata. (ay a-reev-art-a)	You have arrived / You arrived / You did arrive. (said to a woman / girl) – (formal)
Sei (say)	You are (informal)

Sei arrivato. (say a-reev-art-oh)	You have arrived / You arrived / You did arrive. (said to a man / boy) – (informal)
Sei arrivata. (say a-reev-art-a)	You have arrived / You arrived / You did arrive. (said to a woman / girl) – (informal)
Mi dispiace. (mee dis-pee-arch-ey)	I'm sorry.
un po' (oon po)	a little / a bit
Ero un po' distratto / distratta. (air-oh oon po dee-stra-toe / dee-stra-ta)	I was a little distracted.
Mi dispiace, stavo mangiando quando sei arrivato / arrivata. (mee dis-pee-arch-ey, starve-oh mange-and-oh kwan-doe say a-reev-art-oh / a-reev-art-a)	I'm sorry, I was in the middle of eating when you arrived. (informal)
Mi dispiace, stavo preparando la cena quando sei arrivato / arrivata, quindi ero un po' distratto / distratta. (mee dis-pee-arch-ey, starve-oh pray-par-ay la chain-er kwan-doe say a-reev-art-oh / a-reev-art-a kwin-dee air-oh oon po dee-stra-toe / dee-stra-ta)	I'm sorry, I was in the middle of preparing dinner when you arrived, so I was a bit distracted. (informal)
Stavo studiando quando mia madre è arrivata. (starve-oh stood-ee-and-oh kwan-doe mee-a mard-re ay a-reev-art-a)	I was in the middle of studying when my mother arrived.
Stavo cucinando quando mi hai telefonato. (starve-oh koo-cheen-an-doe kwan-doe mee eye tay-lay-fone-art-oh)	I was in the middle of cooking when you phoned me.
Stavo cenando quando la tua e-mail è arrivata. (starve-oh chen-an-deo kwan-doe la too-a ee-mail ay a-reev-art-a)	I was in the middle of having dinner when your email arrived.
luglio (lool-yoh)	July
questo luglio (kwest-oh lool-yoh)	this July

Ho visitato Roma questo luglio. (o visit-art-oh roam-er kwest-oh lool-yoh)	I visited Rome this July / I have visited Rome this July / I did visit Rome this July.
Ho intenzione di visitare Roma questo luglio. (o in-ten-tzee-oh-nay dee visit-are-ay roam-er kwest-oh lool-yoh)	I'm planning to visit Rome this July.
Mi trasferisco (mee tras-fur-ees-koh)	I'm moving (literally "Myself I transfer")
Mi trasferisco in Italia questo settembre. (mee tras-fur-ees-koh een eet-al-yer kwest-oh se-tem-bray)	I'm moving to Italy this September.
per causa tua (pair kow-zer too-er)	because of you (informal)
grazie a... (grats-ee-ey)	thanks to...
Grazie a me! (grats-ee-ey a mey)	Thanks to me!
Mi trasferisco in Italia questo luglio per causa tua! (mee tras-fur-ees-koh een eet-al-yer kwest-oh lool-yoh a roam-er pair kow-zer too-er)	I'm moving to Italy this July because of you! (informal)
Vuoi? (vwoy)	Do you want? (literally "Want you?") – (informal)
Vuoi preparare la cena questa sera? (vwoy pray-par-are-ay la chain-er kwest-er sair-er)	Do you want to prepare the dinner this evening? (informal)
Vuoi mangiare qualcosa? (vwoy mange-are-ay kwal-koe-zer)	Do you want to eat something? (informal)
Vuoi (vwoy)	You want (informal)
dire (dear-ay)	to say
Vuoi dire (vwoy dear-ay)	You mean (literally "You want to say") – (informal)
Mi trasferisco in Italia questo luglio per causa tua! (mee tras-fur-ees-koh een eet-al-yer kwest-oh lool-yoh a roam-er pair kow-zer too-er)	I'm moving to Italy this July because of you! (informal)

Per causa mia? Vuoi dire *grazie a* me! (pair kow-zer mee-er vwoy dear-ay grats-ee-ey a mey)	*Because* of me? You mean *thanks* to me! (informal)
In realtà (een ray-al-ta)	actually / in fact
anch'io (arnk-ee-o)	I too / I also
In realtà, anch'io mi trasferisco a Firenze. (een ray-al-ta, arnk-ee-o mee tras-fur-ees-koh a fee-rents-ey)	Actually, I'm moving to Florence too.
In realtà, anch'io mi trasferisco in Italia il mese prossimo. (een ray-al-ta, arnk-ee-o mee tras-fur-ees-koh een eet-al-yer eel may-zay pross-ee-moe)	Actually, I'm also moving to Italy next month.
In realtà, anch'io vado a Roma l'anno prossimo. (een ray-al-ta, arnk-ee-o var-doe a roam-er lan-oh pross-ee-moe)	Actually, I'm also going to Rome next year.
un biglietto (oon bee-lye-toe)	a ticket
wow (wow)	wow
grazie (grats-ee-ey)	thanks
Andiamo! (and-ee-arm-oh)	Let's go!
Hai bisogno di aiuto Mario / Maria! L'Eurostar è fantastico e stavo per prenotare un biglietto quando sei arrivato / arrivata. (eye bisogno di eye-oot-oh ma-ree-oh / ma-ree-ah. lay-oo-roe-star ay fan-tass-teek-oh ay starve-oh pair pray-note-are-ay oon bee-lye-toe kwan-doe say a-reev-art-oh / a-reev-art-a)	You need help, Mario / Maria! The Eurostar is fantastic and I was just about to book a ticket when you arrived.
Oh, mi dispiace. In realtà, anch'io ho voglia di visitare Roma. (oh, mee dis-pee-arch-ey. een ray-al-ta arnk-ee-o o vol-ya dee visit-are-ay roam-er)	Oh, sorry. Actually, I feel like visiting Rome too.

Sì, quando parli di Roma sei così entusiasta. (see, kwan-doe par-lee dee roam-er say koh-zee en-tooze-ee-ast-a)	Yes, when you talk about Rome you're so enthusiastic.
Wow, grazie! Andiamo! (wow grats-ee-ey. and-ee-arm-oh)	Wow, thanks! Let's go then!

Having worked your way through the Italian-to-English list above without making any mistakes, you will now want to get to the point where you can also work through the English-to-Italian list below without making any mistakes. You should feel free to do this over several days or even weeks if you feel you need to. Just take your time and work at it until constructing the sentences and recalling the words become second nature to you.

the weekend	il weekend (eel weekend)
romantic	romantico (roe-man-teek-oh)
fantastic	fantastico (fan-tass-teek-oh)
political	politico (pol-ee-teek-oh)
illogical	illogico (ee-lodge-eek-oh)
enthusiastic	entusiasta (en-tooze-ee-ast-a)
I have	Ho (o)
visited	visitato (visit-art-oh)
I have visited / I visited / I did visit	Ho visitato (o visit-art-oh)
Rome	Roma (roam-er)
Naples	Napoli (nap-oh-lee)
I have visited Naples / I visited Naples / I did visit Naples.	Ho visitato Napoli. (o visit-art-oh nap-oh-lee)
spent	passato (pass-art-oh)
I have spent / I spent / I did spend	Ho passato (o pass-art-oh)
You have	Ha (a)
You have spent / You spent / You did spend	Ha passato (a pass-art-oh)
We have	Abbiamo (ab-ee-arm-oh)

We have spent / We spent / We did spend	**Abbiamo passato** (ab-ee-arm-oh pass-art-oh)
September	**settembre** (se-tem-bray)
Christmas	**il Natale** (eel nat-arl-ay)
in Rome	**a Roma** (a roam-er)
in Italy	**in Italia** (een eet-al-yer)
in Switzerland	**in Svizzera** (een zvee-tser-er)
We have spent Christmas in Switzerland / We spent Christmas in Switzerland / We did spend Christmas in Switzerland.	**Abbiamo passato il Natale in Svizzera.** (ab-ee-arm-oh pass-art-oh eel nat-arl-ay een zvee-tser-er)
You have spent September in Italy / You spent September in Italy / You did spend September in Italy.	**Ha passato settembre in Italia.** (a pass-art-oh se-tem-bray een eet-al-yer)
and	**e** (ay)
It was	**Era** (air-ah)
It was fantastic.	**Era fantastico.** (air-ah fan-tass-teek-oh)
The weather was fantastic.	**Il tempo era fantastico.** (eel-tem-poe air-ah fan-tass-teek-oh)
I spent the weekend in Rome – and wow, the weather was fantastic.	**Ho passato il weekend a Roma – e wow, il tempo era fantastico.** (o pass-art-oh eel weekend a roam-er ay wow, eel-tem-poe air-ah fan-tass-teek-oh)
preparation	**preparazione** (prep-are-atz-ee-oh-nay)
prepared	**preparato** (pray-par-ay)
reservation	**prenotazione** (pray-no-tatz-ee-oh-nay)
reserved / booked	**prenotato** (pray-no-tart-oh)
ordered	**ordinato** (or-din-art-oh)
paid	**pagato** (pag-art-oh)
done	**fatto** (fat-oh)
the bill	**il conto** (eel kon-toe)

the dinner	la **cena** (la chain-er)
the coffee	il **caffè** (eel ka-fe)
a table	un **tavolo** (oon tav-oh-loe)
a room	una **camera** (oon-a cam-air-a)
a taxi	un **taxi** (oon taxi)
I have prepared the dinner / I prepared the dinner / I did prepare the dinner.	Ho preparato la cena. (o prep-are-art-oh la chain-er)
I have ordered coffee for dinner / I ordered coffee for dinner / I did order coffee for dinner.	Ho ordinato il caffè per la cena. (o or-din-art-oh eel ka-fe pair la chain-er)
I have booked a table for you / I booked a table for you / I did book a table for you.	Ho prenotato un tavolo per Lei. (o pray-no-tart-oh oon tav-oh-loe pair lay)
She has	Lei ha (lay a)
She has booked / reserved a table for this evening – She booked / reserved a table for this evening – She did book / reserve a table for this evening.	Lei ha prenotato un tavolo per questa sera. (lay a pray-no-tart-oh oon tav-oh-loe pair kwest-er sair-er)
He has	Lui ha (loo-ee a)
He has booked / reserved a room for two people – He booked / reserved a room for two people – He did book / reserve a room for two people.	Lui ha prenotato una camera per due persone. (loo-ee a pray-no-tart-oh oon-a cam-air-a pair doo-ay pair-soan-ay)
We have booked a taxi for you / We booked a taxi for you / We did book a taxi for you.	Abbiamo prenotato un taxi per Lei. (ab-ee-arm-oh pray-no-tart-oh oon taxi pair lay)
We paid the bill / We have paid the bill / We did pay the bill.	Abbiamo pagato il conto. (ab-ee-arm-oh pag-art-oh eel kon-toe)
What? / What thing?	Che cosa? (ke koe-ser)
What have you prepared? / What did you prepare? (literally "What thing you have prepared?")	Che cosa ha preparato? (ke koe-ser a prep-are-art-oh)
What have you done? / What did you do? (literally "What thing you have done?")	Che cosa ha fatto? (ke koe-ser a fat-oh)

I booked a table, ordered dinner and then paid the bill. What did you do?	Ho prenotato un tavolo, ordinato la cena e poi pagato il conto. Che cosa ha fatto? (o pray-no-tart-oh oon tav-oh-loe, or-din-art-oh la chain-er ey poy pag-art-oh eel kon-toe. ke koe-ser a fat-oh)
I'm planning to…	Ho intenzione di… (o in-ten-tzee-oh-nay dee)
I'm planning to go back to Italy in May.	Ho intenzione di ritornare in Italia a maggio. (o in-ten-tzee-oh-nay dee ri-torn-are-ay een eet-al-yer a madge-oh)
I'm scared of…	Ho paura di… (o pow-oo-rer dee)
I'm scared of going back to Italy in September.	Ho paura di ritornare in Italia a settembre. (o pow-oo-rer dee ri-torn-are-ay een eet-al-yer a se-tem-bray)
Really?	Veramente? (ve-ra-men-tay)
so (therefore)	quindi (kwin-dee)
but	ma (mu)
I feel like… / I fancy… (literally "I have want of…")	Ho voglia di… (o vol-ya dee)
Yes, I feel like going back to Rome but I'm scared of flying, so I'm planning to take the Eurostar.	Sì, ho voglia di ritornare a Roma ma ho paura di volare, quindi ho intenzione di prendere l'Eurostar. (see, o vol-ya dee ri-torn-are-ay a roam-er mu o pow-oo-rer dee vol-are-ay, kwin-dee o in-ten-tzee-oh-nay dee pren-de-rey lay-oo-roe-star)
I feel like / fancy buying something this morning.	Ho voglia di comprare qualcosa questa mattina. (o vol-ya dee com-prar-ay kwal-koe-zer kwest-er mat-een-er
He feels like / fancies reading something this afternoon.	Lui ha voglia di leggere qualcosa questo pomeriggio. (loo-ee a vol-ya dee ledge-er-ay kwal-koe-zer kwest-oh pom-air-idge-oh)

They have	Loro hanno (lo-roe an-oh)
They feel like / fancy eating something this evening.	Loro hanno voglia di mangiare qualcosa questa sera. (lo-roe an-oh vol-ya dee mange-are-ay kwal-koe-zer kwest-er sair-er)
I need… (literally "I have need of…")	Ho bisogno di… (o beez-on-yoe dee)
I need to speak Italian.	Ho bisogno di parlare italiano. (o beez-on-yoe dee par-lar-ay eet-al-ee-arn-oh)
I need a taxi.	Ho bisogno di un taxi. (o beez-on-yoe dee oon taxi)
I need a room.	Ho bisogno di una camera. (o beez-on-yoe dee oon-a cam-air-a)
I need help.	Ho bisogno di aiuto. (o bisogno di eye-oot-oh)
You need help, mate!	Hai bisogno di aiuto, amico! (eye bisogno di eye-oot-oh am-ee-koe)
I can't stand… / I hate… (literally "I have the horror of…")	Ho l'orrore di… (o lo-roar-ay dee)
I can't stand flying! / I hate flying.	Ho l'orrore di volare! (o lo-roar-ay dee vol-are-ay)
I can't stand living with my in-laws / I hate living with my in-laws.	Ho l'orrore di abitare con i miei suoceri. (o lo-roar-ay dee ab-it-are-ay kon ee mee-ay soo-o-chair-ee)
We can't stand eating with my parents / We hate eating with my parents.	Abbiamo l'orrore di mangiare con i miei genitori. (ab-ee-arm-oh lo-roar-ay dee mange-are-ay kon ee mee-ay jen-ee-tore-ee)
She can't stand working here / She hates working here.	Lei ha l'orrore di lavorare qui. (lay a lo-roar-ay dee lavo-or-are-ay kwee)
I was	Ero (air-oh)
solitary	solitario (sol-eet-are-ee-oh)
contrary	contrario (kon-trar-ee-oh)
ordinary	ordinario (or-deen-are-ee-oh)
I was ordinary.	Ero ordinario. (air-oh or-deen-are-ee-oh)

I was about to… / I was just about to… (literally "I stayed for…")	Stavo per… (starve-oh pair)
I was about to prepare the dinner / I was just about to prepare the dinner.	Stavo per preparare la cena. (starve-oh pair pray-par-are-ay la chain-er)
I was about to pay the bill.	Stavo per pagare il conto. (starve-oh pair pag-are-ay eel kon-toe)
I was just about to book a table.	Stavo per prenotare un tavolo. (starve-oh pair pray-note-are-ay oon tav-oh-loe)
You called me / You did call me / You have called me. (formal)	Mi ha chiamato. (mee a kee-am-art-oh)
You called me / You did call me / You have called me. (informal)	Mi hai chiamato. (mee eye kee-am-art-oh)
when	quando (kwan-doe)
I was just about to book a taxi when you called me. Really!	Stavo per prenotare un taxi quando mi hai chiamato. Veramente! (starve-oh pair pray-note-are-ay oon taxi kwan-doe mee eye kee-am-art-oh. ve-ra-men-tay)
I was about to leave when the telephone rang.	Stavo per partire quando il telefono ha squillato. (starve-oh pair part-ear-ray kwan-doe eel tel-off-on-oh a skwee-lar-toe
I was just about to phone you when you knocked at the door. (informal)	Stavo per telefonarti quando hai bussato alla porta. (starve-oh pair tel-ef-own-are-tee kwan-doe eye boos-art-oh al-la port-er)
I was just about to order a taxi when it started to rain.	Stavo per ordinare un taxi quando ha cominciato a piovere. (starve-oh pair or-din-are-ay oon taxi kwan-doe a kom-in-chart-oh a pee-oh-vair-ay)
so (extremely, very)	così (koh-see)
I was so romantic.	Ero così romantico. (air-oh koh-zee roe-man-teek-oh)
I was so illogical.	Ero così illogico. (air-oh koh-zee ee-lodge-eek-oh)

Is	È (ay)
Mario is romantic.	Mario è romantico. (ma-ree-oh ay roe-man-teek-oh)
Maria is romantic.	Maria è romantica. (ma-ree-ah ay roe-man-teek-a)
I am	Sono (son-oh)
arrived	arrivato / arrivata (a-reev-art-oh / a-reev-art-a)
I have arrived / I arrived / I did arrive. (said by a man / boy)	Sono arrivato. (son-oh a-reev-art-oh)
I have arrived / I arrived / I did arrive. (said by a woman / girl)	Sono arrivata. (son-oh a-reev-art-a)
gone	andato / andata (and-art-oh / and-art-a)
I have gone / I went / I did go. (said by a man / boy)	Sono andato. (son-oh and-art-oh)
I have gone / I went / I did go. (said by a woman / girl)	Sono andata. (son-oh and-art-oh)
You are (formal)	È (ay)
You have gone / You went / You did go. (said to a man / boy) – (formal)	È andato. (ay and-art-oh)
You have gone / You went / You did go. (said to a woman / girl) – (formal)	È andata. (ay and-art-a)
You have arrived / You arrived / You did arrive. (said to a man / boy) – (formal)	È arrivato. (ay a-reev-art-oh)
You have arrived / You arrived / You did arrive. (said to a woman / girl) – (formal)	È arrivata. (ay a-reev-art-a)
You are (informal)	Sei (say)
You have arrived / You arrived / You did arrive. (said to a man / boy) – (informal)	Sei arrivato. (say a-reev-art-oh)

You have arrived / You arrived / You did arrive. (said to a woman / girl) – (informal)	Sei arrivata. (say a-reev-art-a)
I'm sorry.	Mi dispiace. (mee dis-pee-arch-ey)
a little / a bit	un po' (oon po)
I was a little distracted.	Ero un po' distratto / distratta. (air-oh oon po dee-stra-toe / dee-stra-ta)
I was in the middle of...	Stavo... (starve-oh)
I'm sorry, I was in the middle of eating when you arrived. (informal)	Mi dispiace, stavo mangiando quando sei arrivato / arrivata. (mee dis-pee-arch-ey, starve-oh mange-and-oh kwan-doe say a-reev-art-oh / a-reev-art-a)
I'm sorry, I was in the middle of preparing dinner when you arrived, so I was a bit distracted. (informal)	Mi dispiace, stavo preparando la cena quando sei arrivato / arrivata, quindi ero un po' distratto / distratta. (mee dis-pee-arch-ey, starve-oh pray-par-ay la chain-er kwan-doe say a-reev-art-oh / a-reev-art-a, kwin-dee air-oh oon po dee-stra-toe / dee-stra-ta)
I was in the middle of studying when my mother arrived.	Stavo studiando quando mia madre è arrivata. (starve-oh stood-ee-and-oh kwan-doe mee-a mard-re ay a-reev-art-a)
I was in the middle of cooking when you phoned me.	Stavo cucinando quando mi hai telefonato. (starve-oh koo-cheen-an-doe kwan-doe mee eye tay-lay-fone-art-oh)
I was in the middle of having dinner when your email arrived.	Stavo cenando quando la tua e-mail è arrivata. (starve-oh chen-an-deo kwan-doe la too-a ee-mail ay a-reev-art-a)
July	luglio (lool-yoh)
this July	questo luglio (kwest-oh lool-yoh)

I visited Rome this July / I have visited Rome this July / I did visit Rome this July.	Ho visitato Roma questo luglio. (o visit-art-oh roam-er kwest-oh lool-yoh)
I'm planning to visit Rome this July.	Ho intenzione di visitare Roma questo luglio. (o in-ten-tzee-oh-nay dee visit-are-ay roam-er kwest-oh lool-yoh)
I'm moving (literally "Myself I transfer")	Mi trasferisco (mee tras-fur-ees-koh)
I'm moving to Italy this September.	Mi trasferisco in Italia questo settembre. (mee tras-fur-ees-koh een eet-al-yer kwest-oh se-tem-bray)
because of you (informal)	per causa tua (pair kow-zer too-er)
thanks to...	grazie a... (grats-ee-ey)
Thanks to me!	Grazie a me! (grats-ee-ey a mey)
I'm moving to Italy this July because of you! (informal)	Mi trasferisco in Italia questo luglio per causa tua! (mee tras-fur-ees-koh een eet-al-yer kwest-oh lool-yoh a roam-er pair kow-zer too-er)
Do you want? (literally "Want you?") (informal)	Vuoi? (vwoy)
Do you want to prepare the dinner this evening? (informal)	Vuoi preparare la cena questa sera? (vwoy pray-par-are-ay la chain-er kwest-er sair-er)
Do you want to eat something? (informal)	Vuoi mangiare qualcosa? (vwoy mange-are-ay kwal-koe-zer)
You want (informal)	Vuoi (vwoy)
to say	dire (dear-ay)
You mean (literally "You want to say") (informal)	Vuoi dire (vwoy dear-ay)
I'm moving to Italy this July because of you! (informal)	Mi trasferisco in Italia questo luglio per causa tua! (mee tras-fur-ees-koh een eet-al-yer kwest-oh lool-yoh a roam-er pair kow-zer too-er)

Because of me? You mean *thanks* to me! (informal)	*Per causa* mia? Vuoi dire *grazie* a me! (pair kow-zer mee-er vwoy dear-ay grats-ee-ey a mey)
actually / in fact	in realtà (een ray-al-ta)
I too / I also	anch'io (arnk-ee-o)
Actually, I'm moving to Florence too.	In realtà, anch'io mi trasferisco a Firenze. (een ray-al-ta, arnk-ee-o mee tras-fur-ees-koh a fee-rents-ey)
Actually, I'm also moving to Italy next month.	In realtà, anch'io mi trasferisco in Italia il mese prossimo. (een ray-al-ta, arnk-ee-o mee tras-fur-ees-koh een eet-al-yer eel may-zay pross-ee-moe)
Actually, I'm also going to Rome next year.	In realtà, anch'io vado a Roma l'anno prossimo. (een ray-al-ta, arnk-ee-o var-doe a roam-er lan-oh pross-ee-moe)
a ticket	un biglietto (oon bee-lye-toe)
wow	wow (wow)
thanks	grazie (grats-ee-ey)
Let's go!	Andiamo! (and-ee-arm-oh)
You need help, Mario / Maria! The Eurostar is fantastic and I was just about to book a ticket when you arrived.	Hai bisogno di aiuto Mario / Maria! L'Eurostar è fantastico e stavo per prenotare un biglietto quando sei arrivato / arrivata. (eye bisogno di eye-oot-oh ma-ree-oh / ma-ree-ah. lay-oo-roe-star ay fan-tass-teek-oh ay starve-oh pair pray-note-are-ay oon bee-lye-toe kwan-doe say a-reev-art-oh / a-reev-art-a)
Oh, sorry. Actually, I feel like visiting Rome too.	Oh, mi dispiace. In realtà, anch'io ho voglia di visitare Roma. (oh, mee dis-pee-arch-ey. een ray-al-ta arnk-ee-o o vol-ya dee visit-are-ay roam-er)

Yes, when you talk about Rome you're so enthusiastic.	Sì, quando parli di Roma sei così entusiasta. (see, kwan-doe par-lee dee roam-er say koh-zee en-tooze-ee-ast-a)
Wow, thanks! Let's go then!	Wow, grazie! Andiamo! (wow grats-ee-ey. and-ee-arm-oh)

If you've got through this without making any mistakes then you're ready to read the final Between Chapters Tip, which will tell you what to do next.

Well done for getting this far! Well done indeed…

Between Chapters Tip!

What to do next

Well, here you are at the end of the final chapter. You have worked hard and yet a different journey now lies ahead of you.

The questions you should be asking, of course, are "what is that journey exactly?" and "where do I go from here?".

Where do you go first?

Well, that will depend to some degree on what you already knew when you began working through this book.

If you *have* found this book useful then I would recommend moving on to my audio course, entitled "Learn Italian with Paul Noble". It uses the same method as this book except that you listen to it rather than read it. It will help to develop your understanding of how to structure Italian sentences and use Italian tenses still further, while at the same time gently expanding your vocabulary. In addition to that, the course will teach you plenty of tricks that will allow you to make rapid progress.

And after that?

Once you have completed the audio course, I then recommend that you use what I have at different times called "The Frasier Method", "The Game of Thrones Method", "The Buffy the Vampire Slayer Method" and "The Friends Method" – but the name isn't too important.

What is important is how the method works, which is like this...

Once you have gained a functional vocabulary and understanding of structures and tenses (from having used both this book and my audio course), I recommend that you then purchase an *English* language television series – a long one. It should ideally have something like 50 episodes or more (100 is even better). And it should also be something that you have watched previously.

This might seem an odd way to learn Italian but it's not. Trust me. It is in fact a very easy and enjoyable way to develop your ability in the language. I'm now going to explain to you exactly how this method works.

Almost all major, successful, long-running English language TV series will be available with an Italian dub. Typically, the version you can buy locally will have the ability to switch the language to Italian, if not you can go online and order the Italian dubbed version from there.

What you're going to do with the series you've chosen is to watch it in Italian. You should watch one episode at a time, whenever it's convenient for you to do so. And, when you watch it, you're not only going to watch it dubbed into Italian but you're also going to put on the *Italian* subtitles. If you use the English subtitles, you will spend your whole time reading them and will learn **nothing**.

Now while you watch the Italian dub of the series you've chosen, I want you to keep a pen and notepad handy and, when you hear a word you're not familiar with, I want you to write it down. Do this with the first twenty words you don't recognise. Once you've written those twenty down, don't bother writing any more for the rest of the episode. Instead, all I want you to do is to put a tick beside each of those words every time you hear them during the rest of that same episode.

When the episode is finished, take a look at how many ticks each word has. Any word with more than 3 ticks by the side of it is something you need to learn. So, look it up in a dictionary and then write the English word beside it in your notepad. Once you have a translation for each, use the checklist technique you utilised in the book to go through them until you can remember roughly what each word means. Then let yourself forget about them.

The following day, repeat this whole process again during the next episode. Something you'll begin to notice very quickly, however, is that those words that came up a lot in the first episode will also come up a lot in the second. This is because, on the one hand, any words that came up a lot the first day are likely to be quite important words anyway and, on the other, because you're watching a TV series, the same themes are typically repeated in different episodes. So, if you like *Game of Thrones*, you're going to very quickly learn the words for things such as "castle", "horse" and "wench". If you like *Friends* then you're going to very quickly learn the words for things like "coffee shop", "girlfriend" and "breakup".

And it's precisely because these same themes and the same language come up again and again that watching a long series becomes much more valuable than simply watching something like Italian films, for example. Were you to watch Italian films instead, you would quickly find that each film would almost certainly have a different theme and therefore the vocabulary would not repeat itself so much. When you watch a TV series, however, because you're looking up the most important vocabulary and because it's repeated in the series again and again, you really do end up remembering it. It becomes extremely familiar to you.

Now, you may say to this "okay, fair enough, but why does it have to be an English language series dubbed into Italian rather than simply an Italian one? And why should it be something I've seen before in English, why not something totally new?". The reason for this is simple: you will learn far more vocabulary, far more quickly doing it this way. And why? Well, because if you decide to watch an Italian TV series instead of an English one, you will immediately encounter unfamiliar cultural issues – the way people live, where they do their shopping, what they cook – much of this will be different. This means that, if you watch an Italian series, you will not only be trying to figure out what something means linguistically but also very frequently what something means culturally. It will simply present another set of barriers to understanding, which is why it's best *to begin* with something familiar.

This leads us on to why it should be a series that you've already watched in English before. For the exact same reasons given a moment ago, you should try to choose a TV series you've watched before because you will already be familiar with the context of the story. This will make it far easier to grasp what is being said, to catch words, to get the jokes and to increase your understanding more rapidly. Often, you will find that you can actually guess what a particular word means because you are already familiar with the context and this will make it far easier to pick up that word in Italian.

So, once you're finished with this book and my audio course (you will need to have done both to be ready to use this "Game of Thrones Method"), go and watch a TV series. Keep a pen and notepad handy and use it in *exactly* the way I've described above.

If you do this, both you and your Italian will soar!

Good Luck!

PRONUNCIATION GUIDE

A guide to pronunciation is provided under every word and sentence in this book. However, in case you're still struggling with any of the trickier Italian words and sounds, I wanted to let you know about an additional resource that is also available to you.

Forvo

One wonderful resource that should help you with the pronunciation of more or less any Italian word is Forvo.

Forvo is a free service, which requires no membership and no logins, where thousands of native-speaker volunteers have recorded themselves saying various words from their languages.

If you're not sure whether you've got the pronunciation of a word quite right and it's worrying you, then simply go to forvo.com and type in that word. Frequently, you will find that the word has been recorded by several different people and so you can listen to multiple examples of the word until you feel confident that you know how to pronounce it.

So, if in doubt, go to forvo.com and have a listen!